Conten

Introduction

Jeb Corliss was standing on the top of Table Mountain, which looms 3,500 feet over Cape Town, South Africa. He had managed to elude the authorities who frown on interlopers, and he was preparing to jump.

No one would be able to stop him now—unlike his failed attempt to jump off the Empire State Building, when he was arrested by the NYPD before he had a chance to get to the edge. The judge gave him a three-year suspended sentence and one hundred hours of community service. He wasn't going to waste his time helping inner city kids at a drop-in centre this time. No, this time he was going to fly like the eagle God should have made him to be.

It was really just a textbook jump. There would be a six-hundred-foot drop before the wing suit properly inflated, and then he would have enough velocity to maneuver over the massive first ledge. His heart rate was up, but not out of fear. It was the anticipation of once again tempting death and flirting with fate. It was just another day at the office for a professional wing suit BASE (building, antenna, span, earth) jumper who hasn't had a real job in over a decade.

He smiled oddly into the camera and leapt off. In the early days of the sport, the goal was to try to fly as far away from the mountain face as possible to ensure a successful jump. These days the goal is to attempt to get as close as possible to disaster. Today's particular goal was to hit a target balloon perched on a string just five feet above the first big ledge.

Everything was going perfectly; the wing suit was doing its job and Jeb had settled into a nice 120 mph cruise speed. The target balloon was in sight. He would tap it with his hand and pop it, just like he used to at that neighbor kid what's-his-name's birthday party. As he approached the target, it seemed like he might be a tiny bit low, but there was nothing he could do about that now. In the next moment he heard the dull thump as his legs hit the rock outcropping and his body went into a forward flip.

Though he felt no pain at that moment, he knew one thing: he was dead for sure. Even if his legs were still even attached to his body, he would bleed out in minutes. In his last clear moment of thought, he pulled the ripcord and hoped for the best. His chute opened and he somehow managed a mostly out-of-control emergency landing.

Within minutes, the film crew arrived to find him still conscious. He looked up at them and said, "Tell me you're still shooting this." They were, they were professionals.[1] When Jeb woke up in a Cape Town hospital, he discovered that both of his legs were seriously ravaged. One of them was opened up like a can of tuna. The doctors managed to save his life and, more miraculously, they saved his legs, having to graft skin, bone and muscle.

After a year of healing and rehabilitating, guess what Jeb did next? You got it—he returned to South Africa to attempt the stunt again. You have to get right back on that horse, right? However, this time he was unable to convince local authorities to allow him access to the mountain, so he simply found another nearby mountain and leapt off that one.

This story is not some isolated incident of insanity from an otherwise normal life. This is how Jeb lives every day. He has no other interests, does not have a real job and lives for one purpose alone: to jump off tall things. He has leapt off the Eiffel Tower, Seattle's Space Needle, Christ the Redeemer statue in Rio de Janeiro and the Petronas Twin Towers in Kuala Lumpur, Malaysia. In 2013, Corliss made a jump called the "flying

---

[1]   *Wingsuit Warrior: Jeb Corliss vs. The World,* written by Richard Brehm, directed by John Murphy, (New Wave Entertainment, 2013).

dagger." Jumping from a helicopter he then flew through a narrow fissure in Mount Jianglang in China. The opening is one thousand feet tall, approximately sixty feet across at the top, and only fifteen feet across at the bottom. After safely completing the jump, Corliss was quoted as saying that it was "the single gnarliest thing I've ever done…"[2] He told Britain's *The Independent* that he has lost fifty percent of his friends to the sport.[3] In 2003, he lost his jumping partner and best friend, Dwain Weston, when he slammed into the Royal Gorge Bridge in Colorado at 120 mph. There seems to be nothing that can stop him from continuing to risk his life.

Jeb wrote on Twitter, "My death shall be violent, brutal, and there will be blood…"[4] Why would any person, sane or otherwise, repeatedly dress like Batman, jump off tall things, and come near death every time they do? In one word: Passion.

Life without passion is like an eight-hundred-horsepower race car without gasoline. It will go nowhere. It has all the potential in the world but no fuel to move even an inch.

For the record, I don't share this story to endorse the sentiment that you haven't really lived until you have jumped out of a plane or hurled yourself off some cliff somewhere. If you have read my first book, *A Greater Purpose*, you will know that I believe that every one of us should live for a purpose greater than ourselves: to serve others and to make our world a better place. Jeb, although I am sure he is a great guy, does none of that. He lives from one adrenaline rush to another. The Table Mountain story

---

[2]   "Jeb Corliss," Wikipedia (Wikimedia Foundation, February 17, 2020), https://en.wikipedia.org/wiki/Jeb_Corliss.

[3]   Robert Chalmers, "A Wingsuit Diver Died in the Swiss Alps Earlier This Week - So Why Do They Take Such Risks?" *The Independent* (Independent Digital News and Media, September 3, 2014), http://www.independent.co.uk/sport/general/a-wingsuit-diver-died-in-the-swiss-alps-earlier-this-week-so-why-do-they-take-such-risks-9709871.html.

[4]   Jeb Corliss @jebcorliss, 2013, "My death shall be violent, brutal, and there will be blood…" Twitter, February 7, 2013, 2:59 p.m., https://twitter.com/jebcorliss/status/299623540808900608.

in and of itself makes one wonder, but what is even more intriguing is to look under the hood to try to see what makes a man like this tick.

Here is his best explanation for why he does what he does:

"If I die, I want that footage on TV the next day," he says.

"Why?"

"Because this is not chess. This is not backgammon. This is not..." he racks his brain for a more contemptible pastime, and finds one: "... golf. This is dangerous. I believe that footage of fatalities is way more important than film of some guy flying across a beautiful meadow. What we are doing is very important. I believe that flying is what evolution is about. Think of the squirrels.

"At the beginning, there were probably only very few squirrels that even contemplated flying from tree to tree. The other squirrels thought they were crazy. I imagine that hundreds of them died in the attempt. But then, in the end, one of them managed it. Now that, to me, is evolution. And now we are evolving, through technology and through skill. I liken what we're doing in proximity flying to the first animals that left the water. We are evolving and growing. And becoming stronger. What else is the purpose of life?

"Would you ask a bird, 'When are you going to give this up?' Any human being that has ever flown [in a wingsuit] and who knows that feeling, I don't believe that they are going to give it up."[5]

I am sure Jeb sincerely believes that one day he will evolve into a squirrel. And who am I to deny him that ambition? Perhaps I am not visionary enough or have not smoked enough weed to understand the greater purpose in all that. My real point in telling his story is to illustrate the incredible power of passion. Passion is the fuel for life—you will hear that many times in this book. Life without passion is like an eight-hundred-horsepower race car without gasoline. It will go nowhere. It has all the potential in the world but no fuel to move even an inch.

---

[5]   Robert Chalmers, "A Wingsuit Diver Died..."

Every human being has been put on this earth with incredible potential. That is because we are all created in the image of God. Within every one of us lays immense creativity, intelligence and enterprise. When our parents told us we could be whatever we wanted to be in life, those were not empty words. We all have a brain of approximately equal size, we all have twenty-four hours in every day, and we all have latent talents that hold the potential for great success.

So why is it that some of us will go on to ridiculous heights and others will be relegated to abject anonymity? Were Steve Jobs, Bill Gates and Mark Zuckerberg really ten thousand times smarter than us because they made ten thousand times more money? Were Jean Chretien, Stephen Harper and Justin Trudeau ten thousand times more qualified than us to become Prime Ministers?

Were Wayne Gretzky, Michael Jordan and Tiger Woods really ten thousand times more talented than us at their respective sports than us? Though there is no denying the skill of these three iconic athletes, it is doubtful that they were the most naturally talented athletes of all time. There was something else that separated these men from their peers. What all of them really had in common was an extraordinary passion for their sports.

I personally do not believe it is time and chance or even being in the right place at the right time that launches great success, as Malcolm Gladwell argues convincingly when discussing the thesis of his book, *Outliers*.

It's a beautiful example of a self-fulfilling prophecy. In Canada, the eligibility cutoff for age-class hockey programs is Jan. 1. Canada also takes hockey really seriously, so coaches start streaming the best hockey players into elite programs, where they practice more and play more games and get better coaching, as early as 8 or 9. But who tends to be the "best" player at age 8 or 9? The oldest, of course—the kids born nearest the cut-off date, who can be as much as almost a year older than kids born at the other end of the cut-off date. When you are 8 years old, 10 or 11 extra months of maturity means a lot.

So those kids get special attention. That's why there are more players in the NHL born in January and February and March than any other months.[6]

Yes, I know Gretzky was born in January, but there is so much more to the story. Gretzky was a scrawny kid and always played with kids much older and bigger than him. In fact, at age six he joined his first league team a full four years below the minimum age required. A January birth date was no advantage against ten-year-olds. The key to Gretzky's success was that he spent every waking moment on a backyard rink being trained by a hockey-obsessed father who pushed him way beyond what most would think was healthy. His rise to greatness was not an overnight success but a relentless lifelong pursuit of a singular goal—or, in his case 1,016 goals, a record that may never be broken. Here in Canada we have statues built to the man and hockey rinks all over the country are named after him. Even so, how does any human ever qualify for the nickname "The Great One"?

The other stories are not a whole lot different. Michael Jordan got cut from his junior varsity basketball team (I bet that coach felt like an idiot in retrospect), only to practice every night on his driveway to bring his game up to snuff. It didn't hurt that he also grew six inches that next year as well. The rest is history. Tiger Woods has been spotted out on the tournament course practicing an approach shot after dark while his competitors are in the club house enjoying cocktails. All three of these superstars have stood out among their peers because they share a passion for their game that sets them apart.

Golf is the most measurable example because studies have shown that the difference between a great golfer and a professional golfer is only one or two strokes per round.[7] This means that the difference is not skill

---

[6]   Jeff Merron, "Q&A With Malcolm Gladwell," ESPN (ESPN Internet Ventures, December 8, 2008), http://www.espn.com/espn/page2/story?page=merron%2F081208.

[7]   Lawrie Montague and David Milne, "The Fine Line Between the Good and Great in Amateur and Professional Golf and How You Can Bridge the Performance Gap," (Pro Tour Golf College, March 16, 2013), https://www.protourgolfcollege.com/300-articles/the-fine-line-between-the-good-and-great-in-amateur-and-professional-golf-and-how-you-can-bridge-the-performance-gap.

at all but a determination to succeed that stems from their level of passion. I'm not even sure golf should be considered a sport. With the time and money necessary to achieve success at this pastime, it has entered the realm of an obsession.

When Hank showed up one Sunday morning with four caddies, the others in the club house queried, "Hey, Hank, what's with all the caddies today?"

He just shrugged and responded, "The wife thinks I need to spend more time with the kids."

Success in life is entirely relative. It is best defined as reaching or approaching one's own personal potential. There are so many determining factors. Though it is true we might all have the same size brain and the same number of hours in the day, we don't all have the same opportunities. A beggar boy born on the streets of Calcutta will never ever have the opportunity to play hockey in the NHL, but he does have the potential to get off the street, out of poverty and to live in dignity. Few of us are ever going to be billionaires, prime ministers or super-athletes—that is not the point. Every one of us has the potential to live for the greater purpose, to make a difference in our world and to live for a cause greater than ourselves.

Passion is the key to reaching our own personal potential in life, in love, in labour, in leadership, in leisure and, most importantly, in the Lord. We need to stir up the inner passions that will drive us towards that greater purpose and ultimately allow us to become the great students, employees, employers, businesspeople, husbands, wives, parents, friends and Christians we were designed to be.

In this book I will be using the story of King Solomon as a narrative to illustrate the power of passion. As we examine the different aspects of his life, we will be amazed to realize what this one person could accomplish in his lifetime. There is much we can learn from his example, as well as a few things that we decidedly need to avoid. By the end of his life Solomon was remarkably self-aware and transparent about his mistakes, and we can learn just as much from that as from his achievements.

Passion is in no way exclusive to King Solomon, Steve Jobs or Tiger Woods; we are all passionate people. It is one of the key ingredients that God blended into our very complex individual human constructs.

There are hundreds of references in Scripture as to how our passionate desires have the power to order the very course of our lives, both positively and negatively. The goal of this treatise is to quite simply stir up the constructive passions in your life so that you can begin living large in life and love.

PART I
PASSION:
THE PATHWAY TO FULFILMENT

Chapter One

The World's Most Passionate Man

Well, I'm not the world's most passionate guy / But when I looked in her eyes / Well, I almost fell for my Lola

—Ray Davies, "Lola" by The Kinks

King Solomon was born somewhere about 950 years before Christ. He was the second son of the union between his father, King David, and Bathsheba.

That particular relationship did not have a good start. It could have made an episode of *Real Housewives of Bethlehem.* David abused his power as king, summoned a married neighbour woman named Bathsheba, slept with her and got her pregnant. He then tried to cover it up by inviting her husband Uriah back from the battlefield to sleep with his wife. When Uriah, being a more honourable man than David, refused to sleep with her while his men were engaged on the battlefield, David tried a second time by trying to get him drunk, but still, Uriah refused. David then conspired to have him killed by sending him to the front of the battle lines. In short order, Uriah was dead and David took Bathsheba as his wife. This is an extreme example of what happens when we become victims of our own unfettered sexual passions. (We will cover that kind of passion in more detail in later chapters.)

One of the lessons even smart people often forget is that every action has consequences. It doesn't matter if you get caught or not; you will pay a price for every bad decision. The second lesson they always forget is that everybody gets caught. Numbers 32:23 says, *"… be sure your sin will find you out."*

Imagine the murmuring in the household amongst the servants who all saw the drama unfold. It wasn't long before Nathan the prophet figured it all out. He confronted David and told him his child would die, which it did.

The whole sordid story is sad and pathetic and repeated in various forms by men and women again and again even today. It's as if we never learn.

The truly remarkable part of this tale is that God took David's biggest blunder and wove it into His plan for the human race. David and Bathsheba had a second son whom they named Solomon, from whom Jesus is a direct descendant. In that sense, the Messiah—the Savior of the world and the Son of God—came into this world as a result of a sinful and adulterous affair. God's grace is staggering to say the least.

Though he was named Solomon by his parents, the prophet Nathan gave him the name Jedidiah, which means "Beloved of Jehovah" (2 Samuel 12:25). This is our first tip-off that he was called to a greater purpose.

Solomon had at least six older brothers, so the likelihood of him being the next king of Israel was slim. When David was old and failing in health, his fourth son, Adonijah, proclaimed himself king and held a great party to celebrate (1 Kings 1). He never bothered to inform his father, David; the high priest, Zadok; or the prophet Nathan. When the news reached that pesky prophet Nathan, he sprang into action and told Bathsheba what was happening. He suggested that she entreat the King that Solomon should reign over Israel. In a dramatic reversal of fortune, David, Zadok and Nathan together proclaimed Solomon king, and Adonijah heard the news just as he was finishing off dessert. (Judging by how this day played out, I am guessing he was eating pineapple upside down cake.)

Solomon was likely only around twenty years old when he became king, although it is nowhere specified exactly. This young king had an immense task ahead of him. His father, David, had built a significant kingdom, and Solomon had zero experience in leading.

David had big plans in store for his successor. He had wanted to build a house for God, but the Lord would not let him because his hands were stained with the blood of war. The vision to build a temple was to be completed by the son that would sit on the throne after him (1 Kings 5:5).

Early in his reign, one night Solomon had a divine dream, where the Lord appeared and gave him a truly "genie in a bottle" kind of offer: *"Ask! What shall I give you?"* (1 Kings 3:5).

Solomon asked for wisdom to lead God's people. *"Therefore give to Your servant an understanding heart to judge Your people, that I may discern between good and evil. For who is able to judge this great people of Yours?"* (1 Kings 3:9).

God was so impressed that Solomon did not ask for riches, honour, long life or the life of his enemies that the Lord said he would grant him not only wisdom but also riches, honour and long life. Wow, good call, Sol! I can't think of another place in Scripture where such a no-strings-attached offer is made by God. The thing that impressed God so much about Solomon's request was that what he asked for was not for his own personal gain but for the greater purpose and the greater good of others. It is hard for me to not circle back to that, as it is an overarching theme found in the nature of God.

I always like to ask the question; what would we have asked for, assuming we did not have the spoiler alert of this story? I somehow doubt we would have asked for wisdom. The fact that most people buy lottery tickets instead of going to the library indicates to me how they would wish.

One of my all-time favourite jokes on this subject is the one in which the man finds the proverbial Aladdin's lamp on the beach. The genie tells him to wish very carefully, as he only has three wishes. For wish number one, he chooses and receives one billion dollars. Wish two was a Lamborghini Veneno Roadster. He decides he is going to save his third wish for later. He stuffs the cash into every nook and cranny of the supercar and heads off down the road, still in a state of mild shock regarding his good fortune. While listening to the radio, an old familiar advertising jingle comes on and he mistakenly sings along: "I wish I were an Oscar Mayer Weiner; that is what I truly wish to be…" As the old idiom reminds us, be careful of what you wish for, as it just might come to pass.

The most well-known incident of Solomon's wisdom is found in 1 Kings 3:16–28, where two harlots had baby sons only three days apart. One of the women accidentally lay on her child, suffocating it. In the night she swapped her dead baby for the live one. The two women came before Solomon to resolve the dispute. Using his newfound wisdom, he ordered his servants to bring a sword to cut the living child in two and give half to each. The true mother immediately responded, offering to let the other woman have the child. Solomon gave the child to the women who offered to give up the child, knowing that a true mother would do anything to spare the life of her son. Frankly, I am surprised it worked.

It sounds like a dumb government solution to a problem if you ask me, but what do I know—I'm no Solomon! And I mean that quite seriously. I tried a very similar solution to a problem when I was younger, and it failed miserably.

When I was in Grade Six, my best friend was Randy. We hung out every day and did everything together. At that time in our neighbourhood, go-karts were the rage and everybody was building them and racing them at the schoolyard parking lot. Most karts were team owned and operated, as one person drove and the other person pushed with a hockey stick. Needless to say, the team with the strongest and fastest runner won the races.

That didn't stop us from trying to build the fastest and best kart, though. Randy and I pooled our money and built one of the best karts on the lot. It had ball bearing wheels and rake and pinion steering.

Yes, you read that right: "rake and pinion," not "rack and pinion." We literally built the steering system out of an old garden rake. It didn't work particularly well, but we did like telling people it was rake and pinion. We painted it blue and named it the Blue Bomb after the Winnipeg Blue Bombers football club. We had a great summer together racing the Bomb.

At the start of Grade Seven, Randy decided that I was not "cool" enough for him and he was going to make friends with the "in crowd." He was breaking up with me. (This was a good experience for me to get used to, as I was going to have a lot of girls break up with me over the next few years. I was being readied for a life relegated to the realm of the uncool.) Understandably, we had the future of the go-kart to deal with. Neither of us wanted to buy the other partner out, so we settled on cutting the go-kart in half. Randy got the back half with the seat and I got the front half with the rake and pinion steering.

My useless half go-kart sat in the basement for a couple of years until my father made me throw it out. It was easily one of my dumber decisions, and to this day I still can't figure out why it worked for Solomon and not for me. Randy and I were never friends again and our lives took very different paths. First, Randy started doing drugs, then he started selling them, then he began running prostitutes, and so it was only a matter of time until he ended up... selling real estate. Yes, it is a very slippery slope!

Solomon's great preponderance of wisdom is well recorded, as he composed three thousand proverbs and 1,005 songs. He is responsible for writing three significant Old Testament books: Proverbs, Ecclesiastes and the Song of Songs, which is sometimes called the Song of Solomon. The book of Proverbs alone could be considered the single greatest compendium of wisdom known to man. It covers virtually every subject that a person will encounter in an entire lifetime.

(If I could drop a little secret at the outset of this discussion it would be this—if a person had no other resource but the one book of Proverbs, and read it every day, they could easily become a very successful person.)

I have always considered Solomon to be history's most passionate man. To say that he had an excessive personality is an understatement. For example, he had seven hundred wives and three hundred concubines. Or as my daughter used to say, "Who would want three hundred porcupines?" To which I would respond, "Who would want seven hundred wives?" Or seven hundred mothers-in-law for that matter? Seriously, how would you find time for anything else? When would you sleep? When would you eat to regain your strength?

How do you remember seven hundred anniversaries? That's two a day. With one thousand wives and concubines the Bible doesn't even say how many children he had. Maybe he wasn't sure himself. Scripture only names three of Solomon's children. Maybe to list them all the Bible would have to be twice as long.

My mother only had six kids and she couldn't keep our names straight. She just ran through them from oldest to youngest and you would tell her when to stop. ("That one! I'm Mark.") My parents did like the biblical names, though. Four sons and we were named; Matthew,

Mark, Luke and... Satan. I'm just kidding, of course, I didn't have a brother named Luke.

This brings up another problem: How many wives would have had the same name? Twenty-five percent of Jewish women around that time were named Mariam (Mary). So that means at least 175 of his wives may have had the same name. Did he have to give them a numerical designation as well? Mary 1, Mary 2, Mary 3... Or did he skip the names altogether and just number them? How would you like to be wife number 451 or 692?

There is just no way for most of us to even comprehend this. And if seven hundred wives were not enough, he had three hundred spares. Make no mistake about it; there was a tremendous folly in all of this. At the same time, we don't want to miss the fact that the wisest man in history was also the most passionate!

Apparently Solomon did not spend all his time in the bedroom, as his accomplishments are among the greatest of any historical figure. He erected cities for chariots and horsemen and created storage cities. He extended Jerusalem to the north and fortified cities near the mountains of Judah and Jerusalem. He, of course, built the great temple that his father David was unable to pursue. It took seven years to complete, an impressive house of worship built of stone and cedar, carved within and overlaid with pure gold. He spent another thirteen years building himself a palace complete with gardens, stables for his horses and quarters for his numerous servants. Israel reached its greatest size, wealth and glory under King Solomon.

So King Solomon exceeded all the kings of the earth for riches and wisdom.
—1 Kings 10:23

He literally had so much wealth he did not know what to do with it. Silver was so abundant that it was considered as worthless as dirt.

All King Solomon's drinking vessels were of gold, and all the vessels of the
ouse of the forest of Lebanon were of pure gold; silver was not considered
valuable in the days of Solomon.

—2 Chronicles 9:20, NASB

He finally managed to negotiate peace with their neighbouring nations. One of his tactics was to enter into treaties with these nations by marrying one of their princesses. Israel had a lot of neighbours. So many princesses, so little time.

There is at least one fascinating historical connection that can be traced back to Solomon's renowned tact for international networking. I remember watching the news one evening in 1991. Ethiopia was in danger of a military coup. The government of Israel sponsored a huge airlift of Ethiopian Jews out of the country and out of harm's way. Thirty-five Israeli-owned aircraft of various sizes evacuated 14,325 Jews out of the country and into Israel in just thirty-six hours. The strangest thing for me as I watched the newscast was that almost every one of those Jews were black Africans. I wondered where all these followers of Judaism had come from, and what were they doing in Ethiopia? The clue came in the name of the airlift. It was dubbed Operation Solomon. At the height of Solomon's reign, he received a visitor from Africa. She is described in Scripture as the Queen of Sheba. Sheba (or Seba) was the region of the world that now makes up Eritrea, Somalia, Ethiopia and Yemen. Apparently, empowered women predate Margaret Thatcher and Hillary Clinton by a few thousand years.

The Bible describes the encounter this way.

Now when the queen of Sheba heard of the fame of Solomon concerning
the name of the Lord, she came to test him with hard questions. She came
to Jerusalem with a very great retinue, with camels that bore spices, very
much gold, and precious stones; and when she came to Solomon, she spoke
with him about all that was in her heart. So Solomon answered all her
questions; there was nothing so difficult for the king that he could not
explain it to her. And when the queen of Sheba had seen all the wisdom

of Solomon, the house that he had built, the food on his table, the seating of his servants, the service of his waiters and their apparel, his cupbearers, and his entryway by which he went up to the house of the Lord, there was no more spirit in her. Then she said to the king: "It was a true report which I heard in my own land about your words and your wisdom. However I did not believe the words until I came and saw with my own eyes; and indeed the half was not told me. Your wisdom and prosperity exceed the fame of which I heard. Happy are your men and happy are these your servants, who stand continually before you and hear your wisdom! Blessed be the Lord your God, who delighted in you, setting you on the throne of Israel! Because the Lord has loved Israel forever, therefore He made you king, to do justice and righteousness."

—1 Kings 10:1–9

What the Queen of Sheba saw that day took her breath away (*there was no more spirit in her*). In other words, she was completely blown away. Solomon was more accomplished in his day than all the rumours that she had heard and possibly even more than is recorded. The single most important part of the story is that she almost immediately praises the God of Israel, seeming to know that He was responsible for all Solomon's splendour.

Churches that are attractive to the world are always full of people who have discovered a greater passion for the Lord and, consequently, for life itself.

This is a rare Old Testament glimpse of how we as Christians today should live a life of greater passion that points clearly to the Lord God. The people we encounter every day should witness the joy in our lives, the joy in our families and the joy in our churches. Sometimes Christian people look like they have been baptized in lemon juice and then spent the night upside down in a post hole. We, of all people, have the "good news" and should be the happiest people on the planet. I can't tell you how many times I have heard someone say that they would be embarrassed to invite someone to their church on a Sunday. That is a terrible indictment of the job the church is doing of being the beautiful bride of Christ that the world desires to come and see. Churches that are attractive to the world are always full of people who have discovered a greater passion for the Lord and, consequently, for life itself.

The Queen then gifted Solomon 120 talents of gold. A talent was just over ninety-one pounds, or 1,094 ounces. At a conservative one thousand dollars per ounce or so, the math comes out to $125 million. A royal sum indeed! Besides, who doesn't prefer cash over a gift card any day? (I remember my grandmother used to give me fifty dollars cash every Christmas in a card with a nice note. It always seemed like a good gift to me. One year as she was getting older, she accidently forgot to put in the cash and I received an empty card that said, "Merry Christmas, buy your own present. Love, Grandma." It was not intentional, but somehow I couldn't help but feel ripped off.)

Then, as abruptly as the encounter of King and Queen started, it ended with this terse conclusion:

> *Now King Solomon gave the queen of Sheba all she desired, whatever she asked, besides what Solomon had given her according to the royal generosity. So she turned and went to her own country, she and her servants.*
> —1 Kings 10:13

Given Solomon's reputation for the ladies, what are we to read into this? Maybe nothing, but that is not what the Ethiopians do. In their own literature, specifically the *Kebra Nagast*, they claim Solomon impregnated the Queen of Sheba during their brief visit and she had a son named Menelik. He went on to become the first emperor of the Jewish Ethiopian Empire. They even believe that Solomon gave Menelik a copy of the Ark of the Covenant and then later it was switched with the real one for safe keeping. If you study the beliefs of the Ethiopian church today, they are convinced that they still have it and that they are the guardians of the Ark. (And here I thought Indiana Jones found it and it is sitting in an American government archive warehouse somewhere. Silly me!) Whatever the actual truth about the relationship, you still cannot discount the fact that the oldest Jewish community outside of Israel was in Ethiopia, and all sexual scandals aside, you can chalk it up to Solomon's far reaching and profound influence on his world.

Solomon, like most biblical characters, was far from a perfect individual, but you cannot argue that he wasn't passionate. Everything he did, he did with a startling degree of excellence. The temple, the palace, the stables, the gardens, the wealth… he was an insatiably driven man. He lived large in life and love like no other. There is much we can learn from the unquestionably most unique man that ever lived. His accomplishments were spectacular and his mistakes just as stunning. Both serve as meaningful reminders that we, too, were created to be passionate people, called to live large in life and love and to become everything God intended us to be.

Chapter Two

Ted and Bill's Excellent Adventure

Time is the most valuable thing on earth: time to think, time to act, time to extend our fraternal relations, time to become better men, time to become better women, time to become better and more independent citizens.

—Samuel Gompers

Some of us remember *Bill and Ted's Excellent Adventure,* a movie about two addle-headed teenagers that discover a time machine phone booth and travel through time kidnapping extraordinary people like Napoleon, Beethoven and Joan of Arc. Their random encounters not only help them pass their high school history course but ensure that some of the greatest events of history actually occur. It is silly, if not entertaining, and is exactly how real life *doesn't* work.

This chapter is not about those two goofballs. No one ever achieves success or greatness by accident. It is only focused people, following their passions, who succeed and consequently have the potential to change the world.

Ted Turner was only nine years old when he started helping out with his family's advertising business. By twenty-four, his father, Ed, had taken his own life and Ted found himself the CEO of Turner Advertising. The company, which specialized in outdoor advertising, was deeply in debt and on the verge of bankruptcy. Ted moved quickly to stabilize their finances by offering customers big discounts for early payment. He not only managed to turn the company around but grew it into the largest outdoor advertising company in the American Southeast.

Though now hugely profitable, Turner noticed that more and more advertising money was flowing into radio and television and he know that was where he, too, needed to go. Ted began to buy up small radio stations and a struggling UHF television station. These new TV frequencies were not money makers, as most viewers did not own the simple UHF antennas necessary to access the channels. In addition to that, he was running old black and white movies and TV shows that he had purchased outright so that he did not have to pay royalties.

In 1975, RCA launched the first TV satellite to orbit the earth. Ted's little Atlanta-based station was the first to buy time. Then, in 1976, in what might have been a stroke of genius, he bought the Atlanta Braves baseball team and began to broadcast their games live on his little-known station. Within a year, he bought into the Atlanta Hawks basketball franchise, again broadcasting the games. In short order, TBS (Turner Broadcasting System) had become the world's first superstation. He was a media pioneer who reinvented the face of television and internet services for his generation. Within a short twenty years, Ted Turner was amongst the world's handful of billionaires.[8]

He was a driven, passionate man who was never satisfied with an ordinary life. He was an avid and competitive sailor from his youth and, in 1977, Turner entered his yacht *Courageous* in the prestigious America's Cup competition. Although his craft was an older, less technically advanced boat than others in the race, Turner defeated his American competitors and earned the right to defend the Cup against the world's challenger, Australia. Held in rough seas, Turner defeated them four races to zero.

Not everyone appreciated Ted's immodest and outspoken manner. Sportswriters labelled him "the mouth from the South," but Turner went on to silence his critics by proving he was an indomitable competitor.

In 1979, he entered his new boat, *Tenacious*, in the Fastnet Race, possibly the most challenging sailing race in the world. The course runs from Plymouth, England, around Fastnet Rock off the coast of Ireland, and back again. That year 302 boats entered the race, but mid-race a deadly

---

8   "Ted Turner 1938–," Reference for Business, accessed July 21, 2020, https://www.reference-forbusiness.com/biography/S-Z/Turner-Ted-1938.html.

storm broke out. Dozens of boats capsized and sank, and twenty-two lives were lost at sea. At one point, it appeared that *Tenacious* would fair no better, but Turner refused to abandon the race and came in first of the ninety-two boats that completed the course. The 1979 Fastnet has gone down as the deadliest ocean race in history, and Turner's victory made him a legend in the sailing world. Ted was named Yachtsman of the Year four times from 1970 to 1979.[9]

Ted proved that he was a formidable competitor off the racecourse as well. As he made his way into the world of broadcasting, he beat the media giants at their own game. At one point, Turner purchased MGM Entertainment. A year later, he turned around and sold it back to the original owners for one hundred million dollars less than he paid. People thought he was crazy. But what he had done was retain ownership of their vast library of classic movies. Ted had foreseen the emerging market for VHS videos. He began reproducing the titles and made $125 million in the first year alone. If he was crazy, he was crazy like a fox. He then launched the highly successful cable movie station TCM (Turner Classic Movies) to join Cable News Network (CNN), the Cartoon Network (CN) and Turner Network Television (TNT) in his lineup of cable stations.

In 1990, Turner again revolutionized media when his CNN team began to cover the Gulf War in Iraq and Kuwait in live time, via satellite uplink. Using portable gear, his news crew allowed the world to literally watch the American invasion of Baghdad live on their TVs at home. Today, we have come to expect that kind of instant world news, but that was the moment that likely changed the world forever and turned us into a true global community. Dubbed the "scoop of the century," *Time* magazine named Ted Turner *Man of the Year* in 1991.[10]

Like Solomon, Ted Turner had multiple marriages (though not at the same time). When he married the always independent Jane Fonda, she promptly retired from her acting career, presumably because a high-powered individual like Ted was not likely willing to share his wife with the

---

[9]   "Robert Edward (Ted) Turner," Academy of Achievement, August 1, 2018, https://achievement.org/achiever/ted-turner.

[10]   Ibid.

world. In the end, it didn't matter, as she was his third marriage... and divorce. Singularly focused people often make sacrifices in every other area of their life. There was little chance for these marriages to succeed, as Ted was known to not come home from work for days on end.

In 1996, he sold his entire media empire to Time Warner Inc. for a staggering $7.5 billion. With his newfound wealth, he began to invest in real estate and within a few short years became America's largest private landholder, holding over one million acres of land. As often happens with the ultra-rich, Ted began to look at his life and wonder if maybe he needed to live for a *greater purpose*. Switching his focus to nuclear disarmament and the environment, he has used his billions to try to make the earth a better and safer place. In 2000, when the US congress had refused to pay the member dues to the United Nations and was then almost one billion dollars in arrears, Ted stunned the world and paid the bill out of his own pocket.[11] Whether a fan of the man or not, you have to agree Ted has had an excellent adventure.

In 1976, Bill Gates started a computer software company in a garage with his friend Paul (this story would have been way better if it was Ted), and by 1996 he was the richest man in the world. He has held that position for most of the last twenty-some years, with a net worth peaking at some eighty billion dollars. More significantly, he has changed the world forever. His creation of user-friendly software has thrust every one of our lives into the dizzying world of the computer age, whether we like it or not... and most of us like it. Again, whether a fan of Microsoft or not, you have to agree that Bill, like Ted, had an excellent adventure.

No one ever achieves success or greatness by accident. It is only focused people, following their passions, who succeed and consequently have the potential to change the world.

---

[11] Ted Turner, "Why I Gave $1 Billion to Support the UN," Medium, September 18, 2017, https://medium.com/@unfoundation/why-i-gave-1-billion-to-support-the-un-1d9df29a0fad.

Ironically, the two men could not have been more different. Ted is a demanding, high strung, self-centred, Type A authoritarian figure, while Bill is a collegial leader with a knack for listening to others. He never insisted on being the smartest guy in the room and was always looking for talented people to help him build his brand.

So, what is the one thing these two men have in common? (This is a rhetorical question, seeing as I am only looking for one answer, and it has to do with the title of this book.)

Passionate people are often relentless and singularly focused in the pursuit of their goals. There is nothing and no one able to stop them. Few, if any of us, will make the kind of impact on our world as have Ted and Bill (Turner and Gates, not the two dopes in the movie), but that should not stop us from having an excellent adventure. If we can figure out what our greater passion is, that will fuel us towards our life's greater purpose. In the end, it all boils down to how we want to spend the limited amount of time each of us has on earth.

At the risk of ruining the Ted and Bill metaphor, there is another historical figure worth mentioning who also had a similar most excellent adventure. Ben Franklin was a polymath, a person whose expertise spans a wide array of subjects and who is able to draw on complex bodies of knowledge to solve specific problems. He was an author, publisher, political theorist, politician, postmaster, scientist, inventor, satirist, civic activist, statesman and diplomat. Ben gives Solomon a run for his money in the accomplishment department. He was born in Boston and, in 1726, at the age of twenty, he took a trip to England. On the eighty-day voyage home across the Atlantic Ocean, he had plenty of time to think and decided to draft a "plan" for his life. He drew his motivation for his plan from Philippians 4:8: *"Finally, brothers and sisters, whatever is true, whatever is noble, whatever is right, whatever is pure, whatever is lovely, whatever is admirable—if anything is excellent or praiseworthy—think about such things"* (NIV).

Ben identified twelve virtues that he felt were necessary in order to live life rightly. He understood how hard it would be to stay focused on a dozen different values all at once, so he decided to major on only one per week and go through them that way. After completing the twelve weeks, he would start through the list again. He devised a small chart, which he kept with him at all times, that listed the days of the week and all twelve different virtues. Though each week was dedicated to one particular virtue, he would put a dot in the corresponding box anytime he succeeded in fulfilling any one of them. (I am pretty sure today Ben would be labelled with Obsessive Compulsive Disorder.)

The twelve virtues and his descriptions are as follows:

- **Temperance** – Eat not to dullness; drink not to elevation.
- **Silence** – Speak not but what may benefit others or yourself; avoid trifling conversation.
- **Order** – Let all your things have their places; let each part of your business have its time.
- **Resolution** – Resolve to perform what you ought; perform without fail what you resolve.
- **Frugality** – Make no expense but to do good to others or yourself; i.e., waste nothing.
- **Industry** – Lose no time; be always employed in something useful; cut off all unnecessary actions.
- **Sincerity** – Use no hurtful deceit; think innocently and justly, and, if you speak, speak accordingly.
- **Justice** – Wrong none by doing injuries, or omitting the benefits that are your duty.
- **Moderation** – Avoid extremes; forbear resenting injuries so much as you think they deserve.
- **Cleanliness** – Tolerate no uncleanliness in body, clothes, or habitation.
- **Tranquility** – Be not disturbed at trifles, or at accidents common or unavoidable.
- **Chastity** – Rarely use venery but for health or offspring, never to dullness, weakness, or the injury of your own or another's peace or reputation.

It is hard to believe that anybody could be this organized and disciplined, but Ben was. He was so fixated on his twelve virtues that a friend suggested it made him look proud. He was so deeply disappointed by this unintended consequence that he added a thirteenth:[12]

- **Humility** – Imitate Jesus and Socrates.

Ben was far from perfect and sometimes broke his own rules, even chastity, as it became well known that he fathered an illegitimate son. He was completely transparent about his mistakes and listed them in his autobiography. He referred to them as "errata," which is printer-speak for errors. I find that amusing because in today's language we would call them typos. "Sorry about stealing your car—it was just a typo." Though he was obsessed with his virtues, he was matter-of-fact about it when he failed. He wrote, "Do not fear mistakes. You will know failure. Continue to reach out."[13]

It is highly unlikely that any of us could be, or would even want to be, as disciplined as Ben. In all honesty, he is a ridiculous example He invented swim fins; the Pennsylvania stove; the lightning rod; the flexible catheter; the twenty-four-hour, three-wheel clock; the glass harmonica, a musical instrument made of spinning glass; and bifocals, to name just a few. He never patented anything, believing that we all enjoy the inventions of history and that people should not profit from them. He devised ways to keep streets cleaner and deal with waste management. He discovered that the common cold was passed from person to person through indoor air, that prolonged exposure to lead would cause sickness, that electricity existed in storm clouds in the form of lightning, and that storms can move in an opposite direction from the direction of the wind. He charted the Gulf Stream's temperatures and currents on the Atlantic Ocean. He founded America's first circulating library, the first volunteer fire department, the first public hospital and the first mutual insurance company, and he served

---

[12] Project Gutenberg's Autobiography of Benjamin Franklin, by Benjamin Franklin, Editor: Frank Woodworth Pine, Release Date: December 28, 2006 [EBook #20203], p. 146.

[13] Source unknown. This is widely attributed to Franklin in memes and collections of quotes online but never sourced.

as the country's first Postmaster General. He proposed the concept of Daylight Savings Time. He first suggested that the American Colonies join together in a confederation in the Albany Plan of 1734, but it was not adopted. However, he eventually helped pen the American Declaration of Independence and, towards the end of his life, also became one of the most prominent abolitionists working to end slavery. The list of accomplishments goes on and on.

A few years ago, after reading Franklin's biography, I decided I would like to live by those same virtues and see if maybe I, too, could live a life less ordinary. And since misery loves company, I decided to take our entire ministry staff of fifteen men and women on the journey with me. I printed up the aforementioned Ben Franklin cards, which looked suspiciously like bingo cards and worked exactly the same way. Every Tuesday morning for thirteen weeks, we went through one of the virtues. It didn't take long before we got completely bogged down in the archaic language. Who uses the words "temperance," "chastity" and "tranquility" anymore? I suppose I should have translated them into the vernacular: "self-control," "sexual purity" and "chill out, dude!" At the end of thirteen weeks, the cards were mostly empty and nobody shouted BINGO.

All kidding aside, the one thing we all learned was that none of us were Ben Franklin. Who can live like that? He was a man without equal. Nevertheless, it was a great exercise because it showed us all how far below our potential we were probably living.

Life is just too short to fritter it away and then look back and wonder where it went. The stories of Ted and Bill and Ben and Solomon should inspire all of us to pursue our own excellent adventures. The power of passion is without question the paramount quality that can propel us to become everything we were meant to be.

Chapter Three

Time Bandits

Lost - yesterday, somewhere between sunrise and sunset, two golden hours, each set with sixty diamond minutes. No reward is offered, for they are gone forever.

—Horace Mann

Time is one of the greatest gifts that God has given to mankind. It is more valuable than any earthly possession. Money comes and goes, fame comes and goes, success comes and goes, but time only goes. Once it is lost, it is lost forever.

How we spend our time has always been more important than how we spend our money. This is the reason I don't enjoy shopping. I don't mind spending the money for shopping, I just don't like spending the time. For someone like my mother, on the other hand, it is a win-win. The only thing she loves more than spending her time shopping is spending her money shopping. Or, as I like to remind her, spending my inheritance. I remember years ago she had her credit card stolen. My dad claimed he was not going to report it because the thief was spending less than my mother.

In the developing world people value their *money* more than their *time*. They are often paid so little for their work that every dollar, peso or rupee is precious. For the same reason, however, their time is not valuable. I have enjoyed travelling and meeting some of these wonderful people and I am still surprised every time at their unhurried and sometimes painfully slow pace of life. It is probably good for us to experience this and to be reminded that maybe we are far too rushed and anxious.

Even though people in our culture are living longer today than any previous generation, they have become stingier with their time than ever. Maybe they realize just how valuable it is. But in the same breath, it is astounding how much time they will waste by spending it on worthless pursuits. Reality TV comes to mind. Why would anyone spend even one moment watching someone on television living out their life rather than actually living out their own? I understand we all need some downtime, a way to unwind from the busyness of life, but many of us take it to an extreme. We tell people every day just how busy we are and then burn off countless hours on activities that do absolutely nothing to enrich our lives, things like Facebook, or computer games, or TV game shows, or the greatest time bandit of them all—the smart phone.

We sat in a restaurant recently and watched eight young people out for dinner who sat together in complete silence as every one of them was fixated on their phone. It was a "twilight zone" moment because, from our vantage point, it looked like they were completely oblivious to the fact that there were real live people across the table from them. It was emblematic of the absurdity of our information age. Time is too precious to discard meaninglessly.

It is interesting how often we hear the same answer from people when we ask them to volunteer in the church. There is one singular *excuse*, or perhaps, more kindly, *reason:* "I just don't have enough time!" It is just not true. It is not that we don't have enough time; we just don't have enough passion! Regardless of how busy we might be, we always have time for our passions. If something is a real passion for us, we will move heaven and earth to make room for it in our schedules. Golfers will always make time to hit the links and willingly rise at 6 a.m. to get the first tee time. Fishermen are even more extreme and will wake up at 4 a.m. to get out to their favourite angling spot. The computer-gamers, on the other hand, will go to bed at 4 a.m., as they lost all sense of time and spend the entire night storming the castle and slaying the dragon. The Facebook-ers will Facebook till the cows come home and they are personally "friended" by Mark Zuckerberg. The ambitious businessperson will put in fifty-, sixty- or eighty-hour weeks, all at the expense of family, friends and personal well-being. Look around you—the malls are jammed with shoppers, the gyms are crammed with fitness freaks, the restaurants are filled with foodies. We all have time for our passions.

I have a friend who loves fishing. Dean is passionate and borderline pathological about it. About once a year, I go out fishing with him, as I enjoy his company and he can definitely teach me a thing or two about the sport. However, I do have to psyche myself up first, because it will be a long day and we have been known to get back after dark; it's usually about eight hours more than I like to spend fishing in one day.

Dean owns a small electronics repair business that he works at half-time or so, since he is semi-retired. One year, during our annual outing, his cell phone rang while we were out on the water with our jigs dangling off the lake bottom. The call was from a client who was inquiring about a small repair that I suspect might normally have taken a couple of hours to complete after waiting in the shop for a week or two until it could be fit into the schedule. I could only hear the one side of the conversation, but it sounded like it had been eighteen months since his client had dropped off the item. Dean apologized profusely and told his client he had just been "so busy" that he had not gotten to it. He wasn't lying; he had been busy—busy fishing. Right then he had to cut the call short, as the fish were biting and Dean had one on the line. He told his client, who was a friend, why he had to go, and the two laughed about it and said goodbye. It was just one of those classic moments that gets stuck in your mind. Are we really too busy?

There are very few people that lack passion entirely. Most of us have at least one, but usually more than one, compelling passion in our life. A quick search of the word "passion" on Amazon.com recently yielded an astonishing 161,687 different book titles. Admittedly, many are trashy novels about romance and sex, but there are non-fiction books on a "passion" for virtually everything: a passion for gardening, a passion for scrapbooking, a passion for knitting, a passion for computers, a passion for blogging, a passion for sports cars, a passion for pumpkins. The list is endless. We are passionate people because we are created in the image of a passionate God. One day I hope this book increases the number of that search to 161,688.

So, when we say, "I just don't have time," what we are really saying is, "I just don't have a passion for that." Any time a passion exists, there is nothing and no one that can stand in the way of us accomplishing it.

I feel a bit guilty writing this chapter, as I happen to be one of those people with an overabundance of interests that could easily fall into the category of distractions—even if I do prefer to call them passions. I am interested in almost every subject and will read widely on most anything. As for sports and hobbies, I snow ski, waterski, windsurf, play tennis, fish and golf (the latter once a year, whether I need to or not). I love to work with my hands and once built a four-bedroom summer home. I can do electrical, plumbing and welding; I can rebuild motors and I brag to my kids that I can fix anything. I have an entire closet full of nothing but different kinds of glues, adhesives, paints, solvents, epoxies, polymers, and primers. I joke that I should have been a chemist, as I can usually tell you the active ingredients of anything that comes in a spray bottle. Like most people, there are two or three of my interests that are more borderline obsessions than mere passions. One of them is my love for boats.

I come by it honestly. I got the boat bug when I was maybe nine or ten years old. My uncle showed up at our cottage with a wooden speedboat that he had built himself. I thought it was the coolest thing I had ever seen and vowed that one day I would build my own.

A couple of years later we had a big storm, and the following morning my brother and I discovered that a ten-foot-long hydroplane boat had floated up on the beach. By its condition it was clear that it had been lost at sea for some time, as it was rotten and leaked like a sieve. We decided we were going to rescue this craft and make it our own.

Unskilled at boat building, we found a tube of window caulking in the back porch and went to work. Then we painted it cedar red. (Oddly, that was the exact same colour as my dad's new deck). My friend Calvert's family, who lived down the beach, owned a tiny rowboat with a 3.5

horsepower motor. We borrowed the motor and mounted it on the transom of the newly minted rocket ship.

Although the maiden voyage was a success, with only a moderate amount of water coming into the boat, the motor was just too small for this type of hull, which required coming up on plane to run properly. Our dad had returned to the city for work after the weekend, so we were pretty sure he wouldn't mind if we borrowed the twenty-horsepower Mercury off his fishing boat to propel the hydroplane. The weight of the motor on the transom placed the tiny boat at an unstable-looking rakish angle, but we figured once it was on plane it would level out nicely.

The acceleration was breathtaking and there was no doubt that this was a more appropriate repower. However, about sixty seconds into the test drive, we hit our first big wave and the hydroplane broke almost completely in half. Who would have thought that window caulking would not hold a dry rotted boat together? Since we were only in four feet of water, we were able to rescue the motor and nobody died, so all in all it was an okay day. We still got enjoyment out of the hydroplane; it made a great beach bonfire that evening and everybody joined in to celebrate. We knew just how the Wright Brothers must have felt at Kitty Hawk. Their maiden voyage only lasted a few moments as well. Success is relative. Needless to say, the boat building bug never left.

Over the decades I have owned several boats, usually older ones that needed a lot of work. This has allowed me to gain the skills I somehow lacked when I was ten years old. One day I spotted online the boat I had always dreamed of owning. It was a 1985 Checkmate Starliner, an old-school classic speedboat that someone had tried to rebuild and gave up on. The seller wanted a mere two thousand dollars for it, including the motor. The only problem was that it was in Florida and I was in Canada. Somehow, in a moment of temporary insanity, Kathy agreed to travel south with me and let me buy it. When we met the seller part way in Nashville, Tennessee, I could see the craft was in much worse shape than I had anticipated. During the entire 2,500 km drive home, I wondered if I would be having my second boat-burning bonfire. The entire floor and the stringers were completely rotted out and had become a breeding ground for cockroaches (that were now imported into Canada). It had been a saltwater boat, so all of the hardware was corroded out or gone completely. Nevertheless, I went to work on it, and I spent an entire ten months rebuilding it. Since the motor was not big enough for my liking, I sold it for $2,500. I was already ahead of the game. Next, I purchased a late model 250 HP Evinrude E-TEC with just a few hours on it. I was no longer ahead of the game.

The finished product was a shiny, black, metal flake rocket ship that did seventy-five mph. It turned heads every time it pulled up to the fuel dock, which it seemed to have a great need to do. It was my pride and joy and a testimony to the potential of passion.

The big question people always asked was, "Mark, you're such a busy guy; when did you find the time to build a boat?"

My answer was simple. "I had all the time in the world. I had eight extra hours every day—from midnight to 8 a.m.—where I wasn't doing anything but lying around anyway."

I wasn't actually kidding. I typically worked on it in the middle of the night. As previously mentioned, I am not the best sleeper and would slip out of the house after everyone else was asleep to pull an all-nighter working on the boat. Kathy would wake up at 4 a.m. and call my cell, wondering where I had gone.

"Where are you?"

Nonplussed, I would answer, "I'm out working on the boat."

"Why?" she would ask.

To which I would respond, "I had nothing else to do."

It was a long and tiring ten months, but it brought a great sense of fulfilment because it was a lifelong dream accomplished. That is what the power of passion does to us.

So, when we say, "I just don't have time," what we are really saying is, "I just don't have a passion for that." Any time a passion exists, there is nothing and no one that can stand in the way of us accomplishing it.

In the end I sold the boat, as it was taking up too much space in both my heart and my garage. Nevertheless, I tell this story to reinforce the thesis that no one lacks time, just passion.

We all have time bandits in our life, things that consume us and seem so important in the moment but then, in retrospect, are of little value at all. Imagine what things we can all accomplish if we start to arrest the time bandits that steal countless productive hours, days, and years from our lives, and begin to invest the most precious commodity of time into the things that really matter.

I have to confess that I am a bit of a time miser. I approach everything I do based on how long it is going to take. The staff at our church laugh at me because I time everything. I literally time every aspect of the church services. I can tell you exactly how long the worship was, the announcement time, how long someone talked, and how long I preached. In fact, I have a countdown clock hanging from the ceiling that only I can see. I have a few people on staff who say that I am so predictable that they can count down the seconds as I conclude my sermon. I never ever show up early for anything. I try to walk into the room at the moment a meeting is supposed to start. That way I have not spent even a second more at that event than I budgeted.

For me, sleeping seems like a colossal waste of time. I suppose it is some kind of necessary evil because I know how badly I function when I do not get enough of it. This, unfortunately, happens far too often. It seems so unproductive to have to sleep for one-third of your life. My children, on the other hand, disagree completely and consider it some kind of badge of honour when they have banged off twelve hours straight in slumber. When I go to bed at night, I lay there hoping I will doze off quickly because I can't wait to get up and start my day with a cup of coffee. I am so glad they had not yet invented ADHD when I was a kid, or else I would have spent my life on Ritalin.

The concept of time is a fascinating subject. The great thinkers of the past century have pondered its complexity, written extensively and have mostly managed to confuse us lessor minds. Albert Einstein thought a lot about these things. He had a slight advantage over us in that he was a genius and knew a lot of things about physics and cosmology, while most of us only know the few things that we have learned from watching time travel movies and reading comic books. He concluded, in his theory of general relativity, that time was relative and the speed of light was the constant. He became convinced that if you approached the speed of light, time would begin to stand still. His theory has all but been proven. It is an interesting idea because the Bible describes God as "light" (John 1:7–8). In Genesis 1:1, as God put it all in motion, it is carefully worded this way: *"In the beginning God created the heavens and the earth."*

In the *beginning* of what? Not God, for He has existed from eternity past and is without beginning or end. The beginning of man? No, he was day six at the earliest. You could fairly conclude that it was the beginning of the universe (the *heavens* here refer to the sky and space, not the third heaven where God dwells). More than likely the reference is to the beginning of *time.* It all began when he said, "Let there be light" and there was light.

If Einstein got it right, the introduction of light was also the introduction of time. That is when God started the clock, the cosmological singularity in which the vector of time began. Time is exclusive to the universe in which man dwells. Consider this: there could be no end of orders of creation that pre-existed before our world existed. God did not sit around for eons twiddling His divine thumbs. We have no way of knowing about the worlds that once existed before God created the four dimensions of the universe in which we dwell.[14] The Bible is exclusively the story of human history with very little reference to what happened before or will happen after.

I am convinced that *time* is the very realm in which only mankind dwells. *Time* is one of the characteristics that distinguishes earth from heaven. Titus 1:2 says, *"... in hope of eternal life which God, who cannot lie, promised before time began..."* The Greek word used here for *"time"* is *chronos,* which refers specifically to chronological time. This is different from the word *kairos,* which would have more to do with season or era. Chronos is time moving from one moment to another. Scientists no

---

[14] 2 Peter 3:5-7 "For this they willfully forget: that by the word of God the heavens were of old, and the earth standing out of water and in the water, by which the world that then existed perished, being flooded with water. But the heavens and the earth which are now preserved by the same word, are reserved for fire until the day of judgment and perdition of ungodly men."

longer describe our universe as three dimensions of length, width and depth. They now describe it as four-dimensional and have included time as the fourth. That is what Genesis 1:1 is describing. We can only be in one place at any given time.

Conversely, God is not bound by space or time. The idea of omnipresence is that God is everywhere at once.

Where can I go from Your Spirit?
Or where can I flee from Your presence?
If I ascend into heaven, You are there;
If I make my bed in hell, behold, You are there.

—Psalm 139:7–8

It would seem clear from Scripture that God does not dwell in the dimension of time. "*I am the Alpha and Omega the beginning and the end*" (Revelation 21:6). It doesn't say that God is at the beginning and end but that he is the beginning and the end. God most likely lives in a timeless state. He lives in the ever-present now. "*With the Lord one day is as a thousand years and a thousand years as one day*" (2 Peter 3:8). This would seem to describe timelessness or at least some form of time relativity. When we get to heaven, we will join him in that timeless state. Taken to its logical conclusion, this means that when one of our loved ones gets to heaven they won't be sitting up there floating on a cloud, playing a harp, eating Philadelphia Cream Cheese and waiting for us to arrive. There is no waiting, because there is no longer any time. Taking this to its logical conclusion—and get ready for some mind bending—it will appear as if we will all arrive in Heaven at the same moment.

To help illustrate this theory, let's consider the different ways one could travel across the Canadian prairies. When you travel on the ground by car, you can only be in one place in any one moment and you must progress in an exact order: Moosomin, Wapella, Broadview, Regina, Moose Jaw, Swift Current, Maple Creek—those are all real places, by the way. You experience Saskatchewan one moment at a time, one fence post at a time, one wheat field at a time. They say Saskatchewan is so flat that it is the one place in the world where you cannot physically jump to your death, and on a clear day, if you look into the distance, you can actually see the back of your own head. Now, on the other hand, when you travel over Saskatchewan by plane (and who wouldn't want to), you get an entirely different perspective. You can experience all of it at once. "Oh, there's Moosomin, and there's Wapella, and there's Broadview, and there's a thousand wheat fields, and… Hey, I can't see any fence posts at all from up here!" Our perspective of Saskatchewan has entered a near timeless state. We can enjoy the entire province, one end to the other, all at once.

So am I saying that Saskatchewan is just like heaven? Sure, read into it whatever you like. The real point is that this illustration crudely describes the difference between heaven and earth. In heaven, we will live in the eternal now. On earth, we are all trapped in the vector of time. Life moves past us one moment at a time. It never stops and never retraces its steps. In a way, we are all time travellers moving through the space/time continuum at a constant sixty minutes per hour. We have a very finite and limited amount of time while here on earth. We only have one shot at it, one go around, so we had better make the best of it.

As you begin to ponder these things you develop a greater sense of urgency, because life is far too short to waste. King Solomon understood this, and he concluded that there was enough time for everything, as long as we apportioned it properly. He put it this way:

What profit has the worker from that in which he labors? I have seen the God-given task with which the sons of men are to be occupied. He has made everything beautiful in its time. Also He has put eternity in their hearts, except that no one can find out the work that God does from beginning to end.

I know that nothing is better for them than to rejoice, and to do good in their lives, and also that every man should eat and drink and enjoy the good of all his labor—it is the gift of God.

—Ecclesiastes 3: 9–13

Solomon wonders out loud about how easy it is to pursue things that may not be within our God-given and eternal purposes for our life. He claims that enjoying life and the fruits of one's labours life is a gift of God. Time is the essential part of that gift. It is one of life's most precious commodities. Do we really want to let the *time bandits* steal even one moment of it? God placed every one of us one here on earth with a divine purpose, and then He gave us all enough time to accomplish that destiny. It is a beautiful thing to think that He individually loves us so much that he has laid out a glorious plan for each of us to walk out.

Chapter Four

The Passion Paradox

When you catch a glimpse of your potential, that's when passion is born.

—Zig Ziglar

Passion is a two-edged sword—all passions are powerful, but not all passions are helpful. Most dictionaries define passion something like this: an intense, driving and overpowering sense of conviction or desire.[15] Consequently, our lives will move more or less in the direction of our passions, whether they be positive or negative.

The Apostle Paul issued a very stern warning about this to the people of Galatia.

I say then: Walk in the Spirit, and you shall not fulfill the lust of the flesh. For the flesh lusts against the Spirit, and the Spirit against the flesh; and these are contrary to one another, so that you do not do the things that you wish.

—Galatians 5:16–17

At first blush this passage does not seem to make sense. It sounds like the Spirit has lusts, which would be incongruent with the nature of God. However, if you substitute the word *passion* for *lust* when you read it, it all becomes clear. Paul is saying that there are passions of the flesh and there are passions of the Spirit, and these two are contrary to one another. When we give in to the passions of the flesh, they are so powerful that they lead us to do things that we don't even want to do.

---

[15] "Passion," Merriam-Webster Online Dictionary (Merriam-Webster Inc., 2015), https://www.merriam-webster.com/dictionary/passion.

By default, we often think of sexual things when this subject comes up, but it goes far beyond that. We can have unhealthy passions for money (greed), drugs and alcohol (addictions), sports (recreational-itis?), food (gluttony), etc. We have all been to the all-you-can-eat buffet and found ourselves eating and eating until we can no longer move. We are sitting there, with yet another dessert on our plate, asking ourselves the question, "What was I thinking? I feel like I am going to explode." And then we still manage to choke back that last piece of pie.

The last time we were at the buffet, I was coming back with my fifth dessert when my buddy said, "Aren't you getting embarrassed, going through that line again?"

To which I said, "Oh, no, I am just telling people I am getting them for Kathy."

In Genesis 11 there is a fascinating story about early human civilization in the city of Babel. The whole world was together, having one language, and they decided to build themselves a city and tower to heaven.

> *And they said, "Come, let us build ourselves a city, and a tower whose top is in the heavens; let us make a name for ourselves, lest we be scattered abroad over the face of the whole earth."*
>
> *But the Lord came down to see the city and the tower which the sons of men had built. And the Lord said, "Indeed the people are one and they all have one language, and this is what they begin to do; now nothing that they propose to do will be withheld from them."*
>
> —Genesis 11:4–6

The most powerful line in the narrative is when God says, *"... now nothing that they propose to do will be withheld from them."* That is the power of passion! Any time that man has a relentless passion to pursue something, it cannot be withheld from him.

You cannot pursue your potential without passion, but sometimes it is your passions that get in the way of your potential.

In this case, God took issue with their passion; it was idolatrous to think that they could build a way to get to heaven without God. Most of us remember the rest of the story: God stopped their progress by confounding their speech so that they could no longer understand one other's languages. One could argue that He never stopped them but only slowed them down, because mankind has been building towers to himself ever since. Currently, the Burj Khalifa in Dubai is the world's tallest building at 828 metres tall. Trump Tower is a joke by comparison. We flew into the United Arab Emirates a few years ago and the height of this structure was staggering. And surprise, surprise, the building is named after a man, the president of the UAE, Khalifa bin Zayed Al Nahyanh.

Here is the passion paradox: *You cannot pursue your potential without passion, but sometimes it is your passions that get in the way of your potential.*

Aldo lived right across the street from us for twenty-five years. Because my mother was Italian that made us *paesanos*, the Italian word for *'homeboy.'* But unlike me, Aldo was the real deal. He spoke with a thick Italian accent and for many years ran the best pizza joint in town. Later in life, he got a less demanding job as a baker in a local deli. He would go off to work before the sun came up and was home by early afternoon. That gave Aldo a chance to pursue his real passion—his garden. Every square inch of his yard was cultivated to perfection and it made his home look like it was a Tuscan villa.

He had fruit trees and fountains and flowers. He built wooden arbors to support the various vines and creeping flowers. His backyard was a vegetable garden so lush that it could feed an entire village. He would spend countless hours tending his plants and flowers and then, in the evening, he would retire under the shade of one of the trees and sip a glass of red wine beside the bubbling fountain. It was a picture of contentment.

When we moved into our house we had a grape vine over the front door that I was basically killing because I was not pruning it. I didn't even know grapes could grow in North America's coldest city, so I just assumed it was the weather's fault. Aldo could not stand to see what I was doing to it and came over to teach me how to care for it. He pruned it so extremely

I thought he had killed it. It came back with a vengeance and produced incredible concord grapes.

After twenty-five years, Aldo's kids had moved out and his house and yard had become too much work for him in his old age. The house went on the market and a couple of months later we had some brand new neighbors. They were Asian immigrants whom we rarely saw even go outdoors. They spent approximately zero hours a day in the garden.

Within a few short weeks, Aldo's garden was nothing but a giant weed patch with waist-high thistles. The grass in the front yard grew tall and scraggly and waved in the wind like stalks of wheat in a farmer's field. It was hard to be critical since they had come from an area of the world where they do not have manicured, golf-course-like lawns but literally grow rice in their yards. It is possible they had never even seen a lawnmower until they moved into our lawn-obsessed neighborhood.

Then one day I noticed Aldo's car coming down the street. He parked in front of his old house and stared in disbelief at what had become of his yard. I was not close enough to know for sure, but I imagined a tear running down his face. His years of work were ruined in literally just a matter of a few weeks. It was hard not to feel his pain.

Near the end of his life, King Solomon described a very similar moment:

> *Then I hated all my labor in which I had toiled under the sun, because I must leave it to the man who will come after me. And who knows whether he will be wise or a fool? Yet he will rule over all my labor in which I toiled and in which I have shown myself wise under the sun. This also is vanity. Therefore I turned my heart and despaired of all the labor in which I had toiled under the sun.*
> —Ecclesiastes 2:18–20

Now, if Aldo had a great garden, can you imagine what Solomon's looked like? He was famous for his palaces, his gardens, his pools, his groundskeeping, but eventually Solomon realized that much of what he had spent his life on had no eternal value. Was there anybody who would carry on his legacy with the same level of passion? No. In fact, his son Rehoboam managed to destroy and divide his father's kingdom.

Don't misunderstand the point. We should all have time for our hobbies, pastimes and sports. One of the purposes of life is to enjoy God's creation. If we are passionate about these things and excel in them, that is wonderful—as long as we do not become consumed by them. Neither should we allow our lives to be consumed with work. The obsessions with both work and play may end up being the two ditches alongside the road to destiny.

The preoccupation with work is actually part of the curse of the Fall.

> *Then to Adam He said, "Because you have heeded the voice of your wife, and have eaten from the tree of which I commanded you, saying, 'You shall not eat of it':*
>   *"Cursed is the ground for your sake;*
>   *In toil you shall eat of it*
>   *All the days of your life.*
>   *Both thorns and thistles it shall bring forth for you,*
>   *And you shall eat the herb of the field.*
>   *In the sweat of your face you shall eat bread*
>   *Till you return to the ground,*
>   *For out of it you were taken;*
>   *For dust you are,*
>   *And to dust you shall return."*
>
> —Genesis 3:17–19

We were not put on this earth to toil endlessly in the dirt and then look back at our lives and say, "I accomplished nothing of real importance. I made a living and paid my bills, but my life's garden is still overgrown with weeds." Somewhere along our journey of life we need to find a passion for *a greater purpose* (living for a cause greater than ourselves). Too often we are distracted by our worldly passions that have little or nothing to do with our call or purpose in life.

One of the things that success guru Tony Robbins is fond of saying is, "Success without fulfillment is the ultimate failure."[16] Though I am not always a fan of his humanistic approach to the subject, I do agree with that statement. We may not always see it along the journey, but most of us are far more interested in a sense of fulfilment than we are in worldly success. We will take a closer look at this in chapter nineteen. If we were to put fulfillment into a mathematical formula, it might look like this:

A Greater Passion + A Greater Purpose
= Greatest Fulfilment

In other words, the key to a fulfilled life is finding that place where passion and purpose intersect. It almost doesn't matter which one we discover first, only that the two become aligned. That is the winning combination. If our passions do not line up with our purpose in life, they often become nothing more than distractions. That is the passion paradox.

The Apostle Paul is a fantastic case study of this concept. Before he found Christ, his passion was completely contrary to his purpose. To put it bluntly, his passion was killing Christians. No joke! He describes it in these terms: *"concerning zeal* [passion], *persecuting the church"* (Philippians 3:6). Remember, he was the one that consented to the death of Stephen (Acts 8:1). After he discovered his purpose to advance the gospel to the world (Romans 15:16),[17] he turned into a fanatical follower of Jesus that no one and nothing in this world could constrain.

For the rest of his life, Paul willingly endured beating, flogging, hunger, nakedness, shipwreck, imprisonment and eventually death. Why was he so relentless in the pursuit of his purpose? Why was he willing to endure such abuse and hardship without regard to his personal safety? He answers this question in his own words in Romans 10:1, *"Brethren, my heart's desire* [passion] *and prayer to God for Israel is that they may be saved."*

---

16   Bill Carmody, "Tony Robbins: Success Without Fulfillment Is the Ultimate Failure," Inc.com, September 11, 2016, https://www.inc.com/bill-carmody/tony-robbins-success-without-fulfillment-is-the-ultimate-failure.html.

17   Romans 15:16 reads, "… *that I might be a minister of Jesus Christ to the Gentiles, ministering the gospel of God, that the offering of the Gentiles might be acceptable, sanctified by the Holy Spirit."*

Once he found that critical alignment of his purpose and a passion for the lost, he went on to become the most effective champion of the gospel, even excelling the original twelve apostles.

If our passions are fixated solely on self-oriented pursuits, we will end up like Solomon and Aldo, having our life's work overgrown with weeds. Our world is full of people with misguided passions. They consume endless hours, days and even years pursuing things that have no lasting value whatsoever. Our lives are chock-full of minutia that is, frankly, just too self-focused and corporeal.

We each need to ask ourselves the big questions: Are my passions too narrow or, worse yet, meaningless? Is my life a life well-spent? Will I be able to look back at the end of my life and say that I followed the passion that God Himself put into my heart made contribution to the greater good?

Chapter Five

A Greater Passion

Nothing great in the world has ever been accomplished without passion.
—Georg Wilhelm Friedrich Hegel

If you ever have the privilege of visiting any of the fishing villages of Newfoundland, you will undoubtedly meet some of the old salts that spend every day fishing the Grand Banks. They are as friendly a people as you will meet anywhere on the planet. After only a few minutes, one thing will become abundantly clear: fishing is far more than a job for them. No one would ever do it just for the money; the work-to-reward ratio is just too high. No, these men are driven by a love of the sea and a passion for the catch.

I doubt Jesus' disciples saw it any differently. After all, they were fishing on the Sea of Galilee when He discovered them. We can infer from the narrative that these young men owned their own fishing boats and spent countless hours trolling the lake (it is not really a sea, as it is freshwater). When they were not out on the waters, they were on the shore cleaning and mending their nets.

There was nothing wrong with fishing; it was, and still is today, an honourable profession that feeds others. However, the day that Jesus walked by, He interrupted their work and said, *"Follow Me, and I will make you fishers of men"* (Matthew 4:19). What He did that day was to call them to a greater passion. He was suggesting to them that He had something much bigger for their lives—a call to fishing for men's souls and inviting the lost into a personal relationship with Christ. There is no higher purpose.

Notice the metaphor he used for the call. He did not try to completely reinvent these young men but rather redirected their passion for fishing for *fish* to fishing for *people*. For the next three years or so, they fished exclusively for people, hooking them with the powerful message that the Messiah, the Saviour of the World had come. The metaphor must have worked for them because they got very good at it. They not only preached the gospel but healed the sick, performed miracles and cast out demons.

What was equally shocking was how fast they lost their newfound passion when things started going south. Once they were left to their own devises, following the turmoil of the crucifixion, they went back to fishing… for fish! It was Peter's idea.

> *Simon Peter said to them, "I am going fishing."*
> *They said to him, "We are going with you also." They went out and*
> *immediately got into the boat, and that night they caught nothing.*
> —John 21:3

For guys that loved fishing so much, they weren't very good at it. Every time we find them fishing on their own, without Jesus, they come up empty. What do they call fishermen who don't catch fish?—Boaters! Jesus, of course, interrupted their failed venture and again pointed them back to the mission. The good news this time was that they never again lost their passion for fishing for souls. In fact, the disciples lived heroic lives from that point on and every one of them, with the exception of John, died martyr's deaths for the cause.

The greater passion is, more often than not, one directed towards a *whom*, not a *what*.

There is one more critical component in this story that we do not want to miss. The more specific a passion, the more powerful it is as a motivator. As you look back at the Gospels, you will find that Jesus' modus operandi was always to send his disciples to a specific group of people. Originally, it was only to the Jews.

These twelve Jesus sent out and commanded them, saying: "Do not go into the way of the Gentiles, and do not enter a city of the Samaritans. But go rather to the lost sheep of the house of Israel."

—Matthew 10:6

When a vision is too broad, it is easy to lose sight of the mission. In the book of Acts, we observe Phillip being called to the Samaritans (Acts 8) and Paul eventually gets called to the Gentiles, while Peter's specific call never deviates from the Jews (Galatians 2:8). When people say they have a call to ministry, I always ask them the more critical question, "To whom?" The greater passion is, more often than not, one directed towards a *whom,* not a *what.* Once Peter the fisherman figured that out, he never again lost sight of the greater passion of what it meant to be a "fisher of men."

One might be tempted to think, "Well that was easy for them. They lived and walked everyday with Jesus Himself; of course He set them straight!"

Fair enough, but there is a pivotal promise that answers our concerns about finding direction and passion for life:

Delight yourself in the Lord and he will give you the desires of your heart.

—Psalm 37:4, ESV

This is the one verse of scripture that almost every Christian can quote by heart. It is often quoted, well-worn, simple, meaningful, powerful and almost universally misinterpreted. It does not say, "He will give you whatever your little heart desires," as many understand it. The word *desires* can reasonably be translated *passions.* I like to say it this way, "Delight yourself in the Lord and He will give you the passions of your heart," meaning once we learn to shift our delight from the things of this world to the things of God, something profound begins to happen in our heart. He puts in our heart new desires, His desires for us. The passions we will have in our heart become the ones He Himself places there.

Some will remember the timeless hymn *"The Heavenly Vision (Turn Your Eyes Upon Jesus),"* written in 1922 by Helen Howarth Lemmel.

Turn your eyes upon Jesus,
Look full in His wonderful face,
And the things of earth will grow strangely dim,
In the light of His glory and grace.

The things of the earth will grow strangely dim! All the passions of the world that so many of us struggle with—material things, money, pleasure, power, sex, significance—will just seem to fade away as they get replaced with passion for God, His Son and His people.

C. T. (Charles Thomas) Studd was born in 1860 into one of England's wealthiest families. His father, Edward, had made his fortune as an indigo plantation farmer in India before retiring and returning to England. All three of his sons were exceptional athletes and Charles became the captain of the Eton College cricket team. During this time, the family all began to come to faith in Christ, with their father, Edward, leading the way.

In 1878, Charles also made a commitment after listening to a visiting preacher. But he was slow to move forward in his faith, as he was more passionate about cricket than anything else in life. He played on the Cambridge University team and then became the star player on the English national team, becoming a household name in his own right. After his father's death, he also inherited a sizable fortune. He was educated, talented, famous and rich. What more could anyone want from life? Yet something was missing, and he felt trapped between what God offered and what the world offered. He later wrote,

> Instead of going and telling others of the love of Christ, I was selfish and kept the knowledge to myself. The result was that gradually my love began to grow cold, and the love of the world began to come in. I spent six years in that unhappy backslidden state.[18]

---

[18] Stephen Ross, "Charles Thomas (C.T.) Studd," C.T. Studd - Missionary to China, India, and Africa - Worldwide Missions (www.WholesomeWords.org, 2020), https://www.wholesome-words.org/missions/biostudd.html.

It was then that his brother invited him to come and hear the famous American preacher D. L. Moody speak. Charles recommitted his life to Christ and had the intention of serving God with it.

The great turning point for Studd was in considering Jesus' parable of the rich young ruler (Matthew 10:17–23). One day a wealthy young man visited Jesus and asked Him what he must do to inherit eternal life. Jesus asked if he had kept the commandments. The man claimed he had done so since his youth. Jesus did not challenge the claim, like he would have to do with any one of us, but rather, we read,

> *Then Jesus, looking at him, loved him, and said to him, "One thing you lack: Go your way, sell whatever you have and give to the poor, and you will have treasure in heaven; and come, take up the cross, and follow Me."*
> —Mark 10:21

We can see that Jesus was genuinely impressed with him, but we often miss the profound significance of the fact that Jesus was calling this man to follow Him as one of His disciples. It only makes sense—Judas was going to be cut from the team and Jesus would need a replacement. This would have been the first top-tier, number-one draft pick on an otherwise rag tag team, but alas, the young man *went away sorrowful, for he had great possessions"* (Mark 10:22). He placed his love for money ahead of love for his Lord. We never hear about him again. Sure, he probably lived a very comfortable life residing by the thirteenth green of the Bethany Golf and Country Club, but he could have gone down in history alongside Peter, John and James as someone who changed his world. He chose *things* over *people*!

This story was a bit of an epiphany for Studd, and it became his guiding principle. He came to a startling realization: he was the rich young ruler! He decided to sell all of his possessions and give them away. He gave £5,000 to D. L. Moody, £5,000 to George Müller for his work among orphans and in missions, and another £15,000 to other Christian works. In the end he had £3,400 remaining, which he gave to his wife, Priscilla, as a wedding gift. She rebuked him and said, "Charlie, what did the Lord tell the rich young man to do?" "Sell all."[19] They proceeded to give that away as well and started their married life penniless.

At the age of twenty-five, in 1885, C. T. became one of the Cambridge Seven, a group of Cambridge grads who offered themselves to Hudson Taylor for missionary service in the China Inland Mission. They followed the practice of living and dressing in Chinese fashion in order to relate to them and reach them for Christ. Three years later, Pricilla joined C. T. in China. In 1890, the pair travelled to India, where they served until 1906. Studd also served in Africa until his death in 1931. There is much more to the story, as he is still regarded today as one of the great pioneer missionaries of all time. No doubt, he paid a great personal price for the gospel, but in the end he left this world without regret because he had pursued his greater passion.

Just before his passing he wrote;

As I believe I am now nearing my departure from this world, I have but a few things to rejoice in; they are these:

1. That God called me to China and I went in spite of utmost opposition from all my loved ones.

2. That I joyfully acted as Christ told that rich young man to act.

3. That I deliberately at the call of God, when alone on the Bibby liner in 1910, gave up my life for this work, which was to be henceforth not for the Sudan only, but for the whole unevangelized World.

My only joys therefore are that when God has given me a work to do, I have not refused it.[20]

Although inspiring, in a way, Studd's story is not entirely helpful for us. China, India and Africa? This is the kind of stereotypical example we imagine in our nightmares, that we must give up everything and go to Africa to find our destiny. Nothing could be further from the truth. I put it this way in *A Greater Purpose*:

---

[19]   Ibid.

[20]   Ibid.

We do not need to cross an ocean, of course, to discover our greater purpose. If we realign our passions with the Lord's, reassign our gift-ings to God and rediscover the joy of serving others, we will have already gone a long way to finding the ultimate destiny for our life.[21]

We are all called to a purpose greater than ourselves. No one has been placed on this earth without a God-given destiny. At the end of our lives, the only things that will have any eternal value are those things that we did for others, not that which we did for ourselves. Those "others" do not have to be on the other side of the world. They can be on the other side of the town, the street, or even the room.

When Kathy and I became Christians, we were fortunate to have some wonderful examples of people with a greater passion in our lives. One of those people was Linda. She was a suburban housewife who was like a superhero with an alter ego. That was because her passion was for the prostitutes who worked the streets of downtown Winnipeg. All week long she would be a typical soccer mom, but on Friday nights she inspired dozens of people to join her on the streets sharing the love of Christ with women who have never known real love in their entire lives.

It was remarkable to see how passionate she was for these almost al-ways broken people. She would tell them just how much God loved them and that they were worth so much more than what they were selling them-selves for. On many occasions, we saw a conversation, which looked like it was unwelcome at first, all of a sudden take a turn to the point where one of these ladies would be sobbing on her shoulder. If these women had no safe place to go that night, she would take them to her own home. Linda was not going to be satisfied until she got every woman off the streets and living a dignified life. Her love was contagious. There were those of us who came despite being somewhat uncomfortable with the whole scene, and even we saw results. Every Sunday at church, people would be sharing the stories about what was happening on the streets.

---

21   Mark Hughes, *A Greater Purpose: Finding Your Place in God's Great Big Space* (Winnipeg, MB: Mark Hughes, 2015), p. 165.

One Friday, my mother called me and asked if she could come out with us. When we went to pick her up, she was wearing a fur coat and fishnet stockings. I said, "Why are you dressed like that?"

She said, "I thought we were going to minister to prostitutes, so I figured I had better blend in."

"Blend in?" I exclaimed. "Blending in doesn't mean dressing like a hooker!"

Well if she did blend in, she easily looked like the oldest prostitute on the beat. This particular area of our downtown had prostitutes on every corner, so I kept my eye on my mother so I would be able to step in and rescue her if and when she got herself into an awkward situation.

I watched as she approached a prostitute who was standing under a streetlamp. She said to the woman, "Excuse me, I know you are just waiting for a bus, but we are supposed to be out talking to prostitutes and I can't find any. Would you mind if I just talked to you?"

The young woman said, "Sure, you can talk to me, and I am a prostitute and this is not a bus stop." By this time Kathy had run over to either help my mother, or rescue the woman, depending on how you looked at it. To make a long story short, my mother and my wife shared Jesus with this gal whose name was Lola, and that night Lola accepted Christ for the very first time in her life. Her life was a tragic mess—she had nowhere to go and was in a desperate situation—so Linda invited her home and gave her a bed for the night. On Sunday, Lola came to church with Linda.

A few weeks later, she was water baptized, and a few months later she went on a missions trip overseas with a group of young people from the church. She ended up meeting a man on the trip who was in the early stages of going into the ministry. The two of them quickly fell in love and were married, and Lola moved overseas to join him in ministry. That was the last I ever heard of either of them… until about twenty years later. After a Sunday morning service, a woman came to talk to me. She was standing there with two good-looking teenage boys.

She said, "Do you remember me?"

I said, "I am sorry I don't."

Then she said, "I'm Lola and these are my two sons."

In a nanosecond, I knew immediately who she was. The experience of being on the street with my mother in fishnet stockings flooded back to me. In the next moment we were in an embrace with tears in both our eyes. This was an amazing picture of God's grace; this young woman who had been trapped in the dangerous and destructive world of the sex trade was standing in front of me as a beautiful Christian lady with children. That life redeemed would have never happened if another woman named Linda had not had a greater passion.

Let's not forget that none of us are any less children of God than Peter, Paul, C. T. Studd or Linda. We all have access to the same leading of the Holy Spirit as they did. Within every one of us lies a spark of potential that, when fueled by the passion of the Holy Spirit, becomes a flame of greatness. Let's face it, few of us are going to evangelize Asia Minor, become missionaries to China, end world poverty or find the cure for cancer. No, for most of us the greater passion will look a lot more humble and a lot less glamorous, but that does not mean it is any less significant or important.

For some of us, our greater passion will be for the poor, or for the sick, or for children, or for the incarcerated, or for the mentally ill, or for the immigrant, or for our neighbours, or for our employees, or for our clients, or for our patients, or for our students. But it will be about *people,* not about *things*! That is the one single metric that demarcates the greater passion from all other passions. As long as our passions revolve around things—money, cars, boats, technology, sports—they are second-tier passions. People are what really matter in life. The greater passion is the one we have for other people.

Our first and greatest mission field is to the people who are already in our lives. Much of this book is meant to help us become more passionate spouses, parents, friends, parishioners, employers, employees, etc. If we really want to make any kind of difference in our world, then that begins with a greater passion right at home. If passion is the fuel for life and the impetus for all real change, what would our immediate world look like if we became passionate to love our spouse, passionate to raise our kids, passionate to help our friends, passionate to excel in our careers, passionate to serve our church and passionate to change our communities? We would become better people, and the world would become a better place.

Chapter Six

The Myth of Balance

There is no such thing as work-life balance. Everything worth fighting for unbalances your life.

—Alain de Botton

A few years ago, we were invited to a friend's sixtieth birthday dinner. He has a very diverse set of friends to say the least. Some are multi-millionaires and others are borderline homeless. If it was a sliding scale, I realized I was closer to the bottom than the top. Because he is not a pretentious sort of person, he just invited us all and we sat around his huge round dining room table.

I had one of the more interesting seats at the table, since I ended up between Laurence and Larry.[22] Don't let the similarities in their names throw you off. There is nothing these two men have in common. Laurence is the CEO of one of Canada's most prestigious family empires. It is privately held and so there is no way to know what his net worth is, but it is substantial. He is educated and interesting and well-travelled. He has homes all over the world, cars, boats, planes and such, as one might expect. Just managing his personal real estate would seem like a full-time job, and yet he somehow finds time to be a major mover and shaker and you hear about him almost weekly in the news. Larry, by contrast, is a house painter. You will never read about him and I am quite certain he has never been on TV. He really only does three things: fishing, painting and... well, maybe he only does two things. He really lives to fish. He

---

22   For the sake of anonymity some stories of people in this book will have their first name changed slightly, some will not.

owns a little fishing boat with a thirty-horsepower motor and spends every available day out on the water with his line on the bottom. Larry only paints enough to buy gas for his boat and night crawlers for bait. He has no wife or children or real estate. He stays in a friend's ramshackle shack on the lake and is on the water by 6 a.m. every day. You know what they say: Give a man a fish and you feed him for a day, teach a man to fish and you get rid of him for the whole weekend.

It was hard not to notice the ridiculous class contrast between my two tablemates. Yet, both were interesting conversationalists with strong opinions on politics, culture and even religion. It was lots of fun for me, as everybody likes to float their bizarre concepts of spirituality by me when they find out what I do for a living. Now, Laurence's life would be the envy of many. He received a lot more attention at the table than did Larry, even though Larry had provided the fresh-caught Walleye we were having for dinner. But on the subject of work-life balance, Larry was winning: fifty percent work, fifty percent fishing, full stop. Laurence's life, though admittedly privileged, sounded like far more work than most people would be willing to indulge.

Work-life balance is one of the great elusive pursuits of modern culture. It falls right in there alongside other unattainable things like, let's say... happiness—something everybody desires but few manage to achieve. That is because happiness is not a sustainable emotion. As I wrote in *A Greater Purpose,*[23] happiness is based on externals, and unless you can sustain the perfect set of "happy" circumstances indefinitely, which is not possible, happiness will elude you. "Joy" is a more attainable condition because it comes from within and is not dependent on the external circumstances of life that continually ebb and flow from our favour.

Balance is just as unsustainable as happiness. If we ever manage to find equilibrium in life, when everything in our life is perfectly weighted (like on the balance scales of justice), the moment any single factor changes we are once again out of balance. A call comes from a friend in crisis, the boss asks us to work late, our spouse is feeling unappreciated and needs some attention, the principal calls from the High School because Little Johnny

---

[23] Hughes, *A Greater Purpose*, p. 21.

got caught selling pot to other students without a government approved license and tax number—and "poof," balance just disappeared.

Pastor Wayne Cordeiro of Honolulu wrote an interesting article for Mentoring Leaders on "The Principle of the Fulcrum."[24] His thesis was that the key to maintaining balance in life is to simply move the balance point or the fulcrum. When family needs arise, you slide the fulcrum over that way and make more time for them. When work or ministry is in a high demand season, then we slide the fulcrum that direction. On one level, it makes some degree of sense. On another hand, we are still engaged in a constant and ongoing struggle to maintain balance or, perhaps more specifically, manage our imbalance. I don't disagree with the notion, as we all do this—we must. Life doesn't come to us in equal time segments. It will almost never ever look like twenty-five percent spouse, twenty-five percent children, twenty-five percent work and twenty-five percent golf. For a true golfer, the weekend will look more like five percent spouse, two percent children, zero percent work and ninety-three percent golf. Cordeiro suggests we need to rely on the Holy Spirit to reveal when and where the fulcrum needs to be moved. However, for those of us who have missed an anniversary or birthday, we know how easy it is to miss the memo from the Holy Spirit.

Matthew Kelly, in his insightful book, *Off Balance; Getting Beyond the Work-Life Balance Myth to Personal and Professional Satisfaction*, takes a different approach. He claims that the decades of efforts in the business world to address the work-life balance problem haven't improved workers' satisfaction in their work or their personal life. He claims that, as a whole, we are a less satisfied people than we were before all of these efforts began. He sums it up this way:

> In a way the work-life balance discussion has made us feel that we can have it all, and we cannot. Most people don't want to hear this, and certainly our culture tells us incessantly that we can have it all, but the

---

24   Wayne Cordeiro, "The Principle of the Fulcrum," Mentoring Leaders, accessed June 4, 2020, http://www.mentoringleaders.com/archives/473.

truth is, you can't. You cannot be in two places at one time, you cannot have it all, and so you must choose.[25]

In the end, Kelly claims what people really want from life is *satisfaction,* not balance, and that the key to that is to make a list of personal priorities of what gives you satisfaction in life and then pursue only those things. It seems very pragmatic, and there is no doubt that those who have the ability to take a systematic approach to life would find a great measure of success.

My wife, Kathy, is one of these highly organized people. For years, she kept a detailed calendar of all our responsibilities, mostly to keep track of the schedule of events surrounding our children's lives. Games, practices, music lessons, dance lessons, swimming classes, band trips, concerts, youth events… it was insanity, really. The secret to making it all work was to make sure we had no social life of our own whatsoever. Today we have beautiful, well-adjusted, successful children… and still no social life of our own. I am mostly joking about the last part but not about the insanity. The moment our last child graduated from high school, Kathy stopped keeping the calendar and said, "I can't do that any longer. I am sick of living off a list."

It makes one wonder how on God's green earth Solomon "balanced" seven hundred wives, three hundred concubines, palaces, gardens, vineyards, horses, stables, armies, construction projects and the fact that he was supposed to be running an entire country. Just imagine, if you were one of his wives he would only get around to you once every couple of years. If you do the math on his marriages alone, he would have had a wedding every single month for his entire adult life, resulting in two anniversaries every single day. It is really beyond human comprehension. Kathy spent a whole year planning a single wedding for our daughter and I spent a whole year trying to pay for it.

I rather doubt there was anything balanced about Solomon's life. Accomplished? Yes! Balanced? Not a chance! In the book of Ecclesiastes, Solomon gives insight into how to deal with the plethora of responsibilities

---

[25] Matthew Kelly, *Off Balance: Getting Beyond the Work-Life Balance Myth to Personal and Professional Satisfaction* (New York: Penguin Group, 2011), p. 81.

most of us have to face during our lifetimes. He presents it as a lengthy list of things we need to somehow make time for.

To everything there is a season,
A time for every purpose under heaven:
A time to be born,
And a time to die;
A time to plant,
And a time to pluck what is planted;
A time to kill,
And a time to heal;
A time to break down,
And a time to build up;
A time to weep,
And a time to laugh;
A time to mourn,
And a time to dance;
A time to cast away stones,
And a time to gather stones;
A time to embrace,
And a time to refrain from embracing;
A time to gain,
And a time to lose;
A time to keep,
And a time to throw away;
A time to tear,
And a time to sew;
A time to keep silence,
And a time to speak;
A time to love,
And a time to hate;
A time of war,
And a time of peace.

—Ecclesiastes 3:1–8

I don't think the list is meant to be exhaustive. (Twenty-eight things and fishing didn't even make the list?) Solomon may have been history's first great time manager. It would certainly make sense that the world's wisest man would maximize his limited time. He only lived to sixty years old; yet he accomplished more than most would in one hundred lifetimes. What's worth noting is that he did not limit himself to one singular pursuit. He strived for excellence in everything to which he set his hand. He was a Renaissance man long before there was a Renaissance. He didn't say that we should only work, or only play, or only love. Rather, he delineated a paradigm of apportioning time appropriately to the various pursuits of life. Spending a disproportionate amount of time on something will always come at the expense of something else.

His real point is that there is enough time for every purpose under heaven. And those purposes, more often than not, come around in particular seasons. There is only one planting season and only one harvest season every year. Any farmer will tell you that during those seasons you don't think about much else. They plant, or harvest, from sunup to sundown. They are not working on their relationships, investment portfolio or golf game. They are farming full time. There is nothing balanced about it. Come the middle of the winter, they had better invest some significant time and energy into the relationships if they want to keep them. Such is the rhythm of life. As seasons change, your priorities change.

Birth and death are interesting entries on Solomon's list because you can't plan for either of them. Having children, even though we know it is coming for forty weeks, still leaves us feeling like we are unprepared when they do come. Death is even more unpredictable. It comes at the most inconvenient times. We are merrily going along and then someone dies and within hours we find ourselves planning a funeral and being totally consumed by the grieving process. All of a sudden nothing else even matters. Work-life balance is a myth.

The Book of Ecclesiastes is one of Solomon's finest accomplishments. In it he is quite honest about the mistakes he made and reflective on what things were of true value in life. Most of what he gave his greatest efforts to he later came to regret. Tucked away in his prose is the simple but profound statement that what is really important is to enjoy life and not endlessly pursue things that do not have any true lasting value.

> *For what has man for all his labor, and for the striving of his heart with which he has toiled under the sun? For all his days are sorrowful, and his work burdensome; even in the night his heart takes no rest. This also is vanity. Nothing is better for a man than that he should eat and drink, and that his soul should enjoy good in his labor. This also, I saw, was from the hand of God.*
>
> —Ecclesiastes 2:22–24

It's a bit cliché, but he kind of says we should *work to live, not live to work*.

In Scripture I don't see anybody who looked particularly balanced. Was Moses balanced? Not even close! Moses could only focus on one single thing at a time: forty years as Pharaoh's misfit step-grandson, forty years tending sheep and then forty years wandering in the wilderness. The old joke is that they did not have to wander for forty years, except that Moses, being a guy, would not stop and ask for directions. Was John the Baptist balanced? Hello, he was a crazy-man dressed in camel skin, wandering around eating bugs and offending everyone in his path! Was Martha balanced? Seems to me she was obsessed with the work in the kitchen and missed all of Jesus' great teaching, while her lazy sister, Mary, didn't even bother to help and was just sitting around on her duff.

Even superheroes don't live balanced lives. Was Superman balanced? He might have been a pretty awesome crime fighter, but he was an average reporter at best. He was always being called away by the tyranny of the urgent. What about Spiderman? J. Jonah Jameson wasn't yelling at him all the time because he was doing a good job as photographer at the *Daily Bugle*. He was barely getting through high school and had to have been suffering from chronic sleep deprivation from being up all night fighting evildoers and working a part time job. Was Batman balanced? He didn't even have any superpowers, yet he had to run Wayne Enterprises during the day, while maintaining the image of a dashing playboy, and then stay up all night as a brooding crime fighter. That probably explains why his voice always sounds so grumpy.

And finally, was Jesus balanced? At the risk of offending some, I will mention that he had no wife, no in-laws, no house, no grass to mow, no snow to shovel, no kitchen to remodel, no mortgage to pay, no car loan, no proper job, no unreasonable boss, no kids, no soccer practices, no dance lessons, no parent teacher interviews… Jesus had a pretty singularly focused life. Most of us don't.

I might, in truth, be uniquely unqualified to speak on this subject. In fact, most pastors could serve nicely as the poster boys for imbalance. This is because the demands of ministry go far beyond Monday to Friday or nine to five. You are essentially on call twenty-four hours a day, and many people do not know how to respect your personal boundaries. The Apostle Paul went as far as to say that it would be better for us not even to be married. He seemed to think trying to balance marriage and ministry was an unnecessary burden.

> *But I want you to be without care. He who is unmarried cares for the things of the Lord—how he may please the Lord. But he who is married cares about the things of the world—how he may please his wife.*
> —1 Corinthians 7:32–33

In other words, "Boy, I'm glad I can just serve the Lord and I don't have to worry about the old ball and chain." Yeah, I bet Paul was a real hit with the ladies when he came around on of his speaking tours!

Mother's Day is always one of my most challenging Sundays of the year. First, I have to come up with a novel way each year to speak on a subject of which I have no direct personal experience, since I am a father, not a mother. Secondly, whatever lofty things I might say about honouring the women in our lives that day, I then have to live up to them myself because my own wife is sitting in the front row listening to every word. I am pretty much setting myself up for failure, yet every year I do it again.

One particular Mother's Day, I did it especially poorly.

At the time, the church was in probably our biggest growth season. We had purchased our first permanent building in a fabulous high-traffic location and the congregation was growing like gangbusters. We went from single, to double, to triple, and to quadruple Sunday services in one year. The first one began at 8:15 a.m. and the last one ended at 8:15 p.m.. It was a completely unsustainable pace for anyone. By the time the last service of the day came around, I could barely keep my message straight, and after you have repeated yourself four times you can't even take yourself seriously. Most Sundays I would say something that seemed profound in the morning, but by the fourth time around it sounded ridiculous. I would often crack up laughing and have a hard time getting through the message. People would show up on Sunday night just to see if I would "lose it." I rarely disappointed.

It was Mother's Day of that year that I took imbalance to a whole new level. Our three kids were all youngsters and Kathy had her hands full parenting twenty-four hours a day. After I finished my four fabulously inspiring and captivating sermons on the virtues of motherhood, Kathy asked me what I had planned for her that evening. Totally exhausted and naively stupid, I said, without thinking, "You're not my mother!"

Believe me; I am ashamed just writing it.

She appropriately responded, "I am the most important mother you will ever have!"

She was right but it was too late. I had nothing planned and mostly everything was closed for the weekend. I brought home some take-out tacos and it was easily her worst Mother's Day and possibly the lowest moment in our marriage. In fact, it was the beginning of our worst year ever. It did not take me long to realize that I was the problem and that my life was so profoundly out of balance that I was sacrificing my family on the altar of ministry. Others do the same on the altar of work, sports, fishing, gambling, cars and motorcycles, etc.

After our Mother's Day marriage meltdown, I realized I had allowed my passion to serve the mission of the church to monopolize all my time. I loved my wife and children dearly but had begun to take my family for granted, assuming that if I was doing God's work then everything else should take care of itself. Right? Wrong! The things that God has entrusted us with require our attention. I recognized my inattentiveness and decided I was going to be the best husband, best father and the best pastor I could be. God does not entrust to us more than we can handle, but we must rely on His strength, not our own!

Not that we are sufficient of ourselves to think of anything as being from ourselves, but our sufficiency is from God.
—2 Corinthians 3:5

And God is able to make all grace abound toward you, that you, always having all sufficiency in all things, may have an abundance for every good work.
—2 Corinthians 9:8

People find time for their passions. If I am passionate for my wife, I will have time for her. If I am passionate for my kids, I will have time for them. It took some time to get there, but over the following months Kathy began to notice that my attention for them had risen substantially, and within a year our family life was in a much better place. I still had to work long hours, but I was diligent to reduce the number of evening meetings and I made getting home for dinner a priority. I started travelling much less. I endeavoured to make sure I was at soccer games and band concerts. Did I make every one of them? No, but I didn't miss every one of them either. Did the church suffer? Of course not. It is not one hundred percent dependent on me.

People are knocking themselves out trying to achieve the perfect balancing point, but it is an unachievable moving target. We don't need to be balanced people—we need to be passionate people,

A leader's sense of self-importance is what stifles most organizations. Moses learned this lesson the hard way while he was leading the children of Israel out of Egypt. In Exodus 18, we see they had come to a complete standstill, as Moses spent all day, every day, judging the people. They would line up and he would dole out his self-perceived great wisdom. His father-in-law, Jethro, was watching this scene play out and finally came over to confront him: "Moses, you are an idiot… this thing that you are doing is not good!" I am paraphrasing only slightly, but you know how fathers-in-law can talk to their sons-in-law! He tells Moses that he is going to wear himself and the people out. Jethro suggests, instead, a new model of leadership, with rulers of thousands, rulers of hundreds, rulers of fifties and rulers of tens. There were smart people in their midst who could judge for themselves and Moses could deal then with only the difficult matters. This delegated approach solved the logjam and they were once again able to move forward. Many of us as leaders fail to realize that our sense of indispensability is, in fact, the problem. Most of us need to work smarter, not harder. No one ever said on their deathbed, "I wish I had spent more time at the office."[26]

This whole journey helped me become a better family man and a better pastor. There was really no way to balance a scenario as demanding as what we were trying to live. This is the modern dilemma. People are knocking themselves out trying to achieve the perfect balancing point, but it is an unachievable moving target.

We don't need to be balanced people—we need to be passionate people, passionate not just in a couple of things like work and sports but in the larger complement of truly important things of life: passion for God, passion for our spouse, passion for our kids, passion for our friends, passion for our jobs and a passion to live for a purpose greater than ourselves.

So now, when we look for leaders in the church, we don't look for the so-called balanced people. They are often the ones who use the work-life balance as an excuse to say no. When we look for leaders these days, we

---

[26]   Ralph Keyes, *The Quote Verifier: Who Said What, Where, and When* (New York: St. Martin's Press/Macmillan, 2006), p. 42. In the early 1980s, a Massachusetts lawyer named Arnold Zack made this observation to his friend Paul Tsongas. Tsongas, then a U.S. senator, was suffering from the lymphoma that eventually killed him. Zack believes the thought was original to him. Tsongas recorded his friend's observation in a 1984 book. Today this popular maxim is usually quoted as "No one on his deathbed ever said, 'I wish I had spent more time at the office."

look for passionate people because they will find time for work, family, God and church. The best volunteer leaders we have in the church are, not surprisingly, also the best spouses and parents!

PART II
LIVING LARGE
IN LIFE AND LOVE

Chapter Seven

A Marriage License Is Only a Learner's Permit

By all means marry; if you get a good wife, you'll become happy; if you get a bad one, you'll become a philosopher.

—Socrates

Someone once said, "Love is blind but marriage is an eye-opener." One day you are free and single; the next, you have committed to spending every single day for the rest of your life with the same person.

Nobody really knows what they are getting into when they get married. When a young person is learning how to drive a car, they start with a learner's permit. They don't give them a full license until they have passed both a written and driving road test and the examiner is confident they are no longer a menace on the road. Marriage is the opposite—you get a license by merely saying "I do" and then you become a menace on the road of life.

A Grade Three teacher was curious to discover what her young pupils knew about love and romance. She asked the class the simple question: What is love?

Eight-year-old Mae confidently explained. "It is when Daddy comes home work all smelly and mommy still gives him a kiss anyway."

Nine-year-old Lilly offered her sage wisdom: "No one knows for sure, but I have heard it has something to do with how you smell—it is why perfume and deodorant are so popular."

The boys were a little less romantic, with Josh explaining, "Nobody know for sure, but I think you get shot with an arrow and is very painful."

Andrew thought he had a better answer. "It is like an avalanche where you have to run for your life."

As we look at the life of King Solomon, we do not want to assume that, just because he was smart, he was also always right. If we have learned one thing from history, it is that smart people are not immune from doing stupid things. The issue of the aforementioned seven hundred wives and three hundred concubines comes to mind.

In Deuteronomy 17, Moses warned Israel that, after they came into the Promised Land, one day they would have a king. He went on to give them some very specific instructions about the king's conduct.

> *But he shall not multiply horses for himself, nor cause the people to return to Egypt to multiply horses, for the Lord has said to you, "You shall not return that way again." Neither shall he multiply wives for himself, lest his heart turn away; nor shall he greatly multiply silver and gold for himself.*
> —Deuteronomy 17:16–17

Not too many horses, not too much gold and silver and not too many wives? How did our good King Solomon do on those three counts? Fail, fail, fail! We will look at the horses, gold and silver later, but for now we will concentrate on the wives.

One of the big questions Christian people often ask is this: Why did God allow polygamy in the Old Testament? We do not want to confuse the word "allow" with "approve." Even King Solomon's own advice on marriage seems to belie his behaviour. *"He who finds a wife finds a good thing, and obtains favor from the Lord"* (Proverbs 18:22). Perhaps his logic was that if one wife is a *good* thing, then seven hundred wives must be an *awesome* thing! Well, we'll see about that. Solomon's own book of wisdom seems to speak of the exclusivity of marriage. To find and keep that singular bride of one's youth is perhaps life's greatest blessing from God.

> *Let your fountain be blessed,*
> *And rejoice with the wife of your youth.*
> —Proverbs 5:18

An excellent wife is the crown of her husband...

—Proverbs 12:4a

Houses and riches are an inheritance from fathers,
But a prudent wife is from the Lord.

—Proverbs 19:14

Who can find a virtuous wife?
For her worth is far above rubies.

—Proverbs 31:10

In the New Testament it is even clearer that the "approved" number of wives is one. Instructions in 1 Timothy 3:2, 3:12 and Titus 1:6 require being *"the husband of one wife"* in a list of qualifications for spiritual leadership. One could make a reasonable argument that the Old Testament does not specifically prohibit multiple marriages, but it certainly doesn't endorse it. Most of the time, when polygamy is mentioned in Scripture it does so in terms of the problems that it creates.

There is an old joke about this. Question: What is the penalty today for bigamy in Canada? Answer: Two wives!

Notwithstanding all of King Solomon's extraordinary accomplishments, his proclivity for a multiplicity of wives was without question his worst personal example. There is no question that, in terms of sheer quantity of wives and concubines, he wins, but in terms of loyalty, he had fidelity of an alley cat. If you were in his harem, the math would suggest that your turn would come around once every three years. Yippee, right? However, I would be very surprised if he slept with them on a rotating basis. Chances are, once he had married one and slept with her for a few days or weeks, his eye would wander and he would be on to the next one. Then his last wife would then we relegated to the back bedroom of the zenana residence while Casanova moved on to a younger, prettier model.

If we look at powerful men today who have married multiple times, they never move on to an older, dowdier wife. When Hugh Hefner died at ninety-one, his current girlfriend was in her twenties. For many years,

Hef had three concurrent live-in girlfriends and they all shared a single bed together. He jealously controlled their lives by imposing a 9 p.m. curfew so that he could ensure they would not stray. Meanwhile, he was free to sleep with whoever he wished. It was reported that he had been with over one thousand women.[27] Hugh Hefner is portrayed by the media as a champion of women's rights; yet he did more to enslave and objectify them than almost any man in the twentieth century.

I fail to see how Solomon's example was any different than the likes of the founder of *Playboy* magazine. That kind of behaviour can't be God's intention. These women would be completely starved for any emotional support from their husband. It is certain that they would have had lots of "girlfriend time," but they probably spent most of it complaining about oversexed Sol. Personally, whether it was technically un-sinful or not, I find the whole idea of Solomon's marital excessiveness more than a bit despicable.

At first blush, one might conclude the discussion of polygamy is a moot point, as almost no one practices it in our culture today. But, in fact, we surely do—we just do it (mostly) one spouse at a time. In the West, the vast majority of people today have multiple partners before, after, or unfortunately, during marriage. The average age for a North American teen to become sexually active is seventeen years old, a full decade before most will be married. Cultural anthropologists claim that we come by this naturally, as there are only a handful of mammals that are monogamous. Most animals are like the infidel junkyard dog that will mate with whatever partner happens to be around. Behavioral scientists have concluded that, because mankind is just another animal, we are not genetically predisposed to monogamy.[28] (As we have seen, the Bible has something different to say about this.) Although there are only a few examples of monogamous mammals—gibbons, beavers, wolves and killer whales—there

---

[27] Kirsten Acuna, "A Guide to Hugh Hefner's Many Gorgeous Wives and Girlfriends through the Years," *Insider*, September 28, 2017, https://www.insider.com/hugh-hefner-wives-girl-friends-list-2017-9.

[28] E. E. Smith, "Monogamy Is Not 'Natural' For Human Beings," *Psychology Today* (Sussex Publishers, May 20, 2016), https://www.psychologytoday.com/ca/blog/not-born-yester-day/201605/monogamy-is-not-natural-human-beings.

are many birds that practice monogamy and only choose one mate for an entire lifetime.

We have had a pair of pet loons for about twenty years. Well, "pet" might be an overstatement. This mating couple has called the waters directly in front of our lake cottage their summer home for the last two decades. Every summer they return to exactly the same spot right in front of our dock. They float around together all day and cry eerily and loudly back and forth all night long. We have fallen in love with our loons. They have become completely oblivious to our presence and will barely move out of the way when we go by in the boat.

They are stunningly beautiful creatures in all-black-and-white with red eyes. We have watched with a bit of heartbreak as Stan and Shirley[29] have tried to procreate. (We could never tell for sure which one was Stan and which one was Shirley—they all look alike.) Loons will lay only one or two eggs and will do so right at the water's edge, which can be a hostile marine environment with storm waves or natural predators. There have been only a few years where they have managed to hatch an egg. The mother will go to great lengths to guard the new chick, carrying it on its back for the first couple of weeks. Once the chick can swim, the parents will float very nearby.

Tragically, it seems like every year a bald eagle or muskellunge fish manages to pick off the young one. One summer, however, we had a breakthrough. We not only cheered for the newly hatched chick but prayed that it would survive. Finally, after twenty years our pet loons had their first offspring survive, and in the fall they all flew off together.

I am not sure birds can sense heartache, but we felt for them all those years. So, it was not really surprising how much personal joy it brought to watch the faithful loon couple finally experience success. We have become emotionally invested in our loons.

We feel the same way when we cheer on married people to succeed in a world that can only be considered a hostile environment. Tax laws no longer favour married people. Divorce laws make it easier than ever

---

[29] We borrowed the name Shirley from the Warner Bros *Tiny Toons* cartoon character Shirley McLoon. You would need to have young children to know.

to end a marriage that began with the words, "Till death do we part." Everything within our culture conspires against marriage. Pop culture presents marriage as more of an inconvenience than a sacred blessing. Movies, television and popular literature present to our young people a version of relationship that begins with hooking up, followed by living together and then only an outside chance of ending up in an actual marriage.

Cultural icon Oprah has lived together with Stedman Graham for over thirty years with no apparent sense of compunction, nor any intention to ever marry. Mick Jagger fathered eight children from five different women and was only ever married to one of them. He was seventy-two when he had his last child, almost as old as Abraham! Like Solomon, he just kept trading them in on a newer model… literally, as most of Jagger's girlfriends and wife Jerry Hall were supermodels.

The birth rate outside of marriage has reached a shocking level. Among African Americans, a staggering seventy-three percent of children are born out of wedlock. Of Hispanic Americans it is sixty-three percent.

In the province of Quebec, Canada, it is also sixty-three percent.[30] What is disheartening about this is that Quebec was a predominately Catholic province where, for generations, abortion, illegitimate children and divorce were almost unheard of.

Prior to 1960, almost all Quebecers were practicing Catholics. Cities like Montreal are dotted with some of the most beautiful churches and cathedrals in the world. Beginning in the 1960s, the Quebec government led the way in what became known as the Quiet Revolution. It was a massive, systematic move towards the secularization of the province. Lawmakers jettisoned what they considered archaic legislation that was rooted in Catholic morality. Quebecers embarked on a mass abandonment of religion and left it in the past. Churches were turned into night clubs and condos.

As Dr. Phil would say, "How's that working for you?" Well, today the province has the highest abortion, suicide and illegitimate birth rates in

---

[30] "Proportion of Births Outside Marriage by Birth Order, Quebec, 1976-2019," Proportion de naissances hors mariage selon le rang de naissance, Québec, 1976-2019 (Institut de la Statistique du Québec, April 29, 2020), http://www.stat.gouv.qc.ca/statistiques/population-demographie/naissance-fecondite/5p2.htm.

Canada. On the statistical upside, the divorce rate is the lowest in Canada… but only because so few young people are actually getting married.[31]

Irrespective of what may be happening with the institution of marriage around us, it was and still is God's best ideal. Notwithstanding the difficulties of marriage, people who are passionate about their spouses can overcome these challenges with great prevailing success.

Dietrich Bonhoeffer, the great German Pastor who was executed by the Nazis during WWII, made this spectacular claim: "It is not your love that will sustain your marriage, but your marriage that will sustain your love[32]." Bonhoeffer understood that the so-called *feelings of love* will almost certainly ebb and flow in any marital relationship. No one will ever be able to live up to the Hollywood expectations that true love is somehow a lifetime of sustained emotional mountaintop experiences.

Everybody struggles with the feelings; it goes with the territory. Billy Graham's wife, Ruth Graham, was once asked if she had ever considered divorce. She wryly responded, "Divorce, never. Murder, many times, but never divorce."[33] What Bonhoeffer was suggesting is that marriage is a choice that transcends the emotional roller coaster that we call love. He was referring to the miracle of marriage.

Jesus said, *"For this reason a man shall leave his father and mother and be joined to his wife, and the two shall become one flesh"*(Matthew 19:5). When two people agree to matrimony and say, "I do," they are making a lifelong decision to stay together for richer or poorer, for better or worse, through sickness or health, till death do they part. God Himself is in the midst of that decision to perform a miracle to join the two together as one flesh. The idea of a one flesh relationship is profound; somehow two unique people can bring their separate lives together into one. How could that not be fraught with difficulties?

---

[31] "Province of Quebec," Focus on Geography Series, 2016 Census (Statistics Canada, April 10, 2019), https://www12.statcan.gc.ca/census-recensement/2016/as-sa/fogs-spg/Facts-PR-Eng.cfm?TOPIC=4&LANG=Eng&GK=PR&GC=24.

[32] Ryan Frederick, "A Wedding Sermon from a 1943 Prison Cell ," Fierce Marriage, July 9, 2018, https://fiercemarriage.com/a-wedding-sermon-from-a-1943-prison-cell-dietrich-bonhoeffer.

[33] Nancy Gibbs and Michael Duffy, "Ruth Graham, Soulmate to Billy, Dies," *Time* (Time Inc., June 14, 2007), http://content.time.com/time/nation/article/0,8599,1633197,00.html.

The Apostle Paul, although he did not seem to be married, offered possibly the single greatest marital advice ever recorded. It can be found in Ephesians 5:33: *"Nevertheless let each one of you in particular so love his own wife as himself, and let the wife see that she respects her husband."* If you read the whole chapter you will discover that he tells husbands three times to *love* their wives. And yet he does not tell wives to do the same but rather implores them to *respect* their husbands. I always joke with the women that they are under no obligation to love their husbands—who could love these hairy, sweaty, uncouth beasts anyway?

But there is a hidden truth here that we do not want to miss. Paul is addressing the most common singular needs of the male and female psyche. For most women the need to be loved, cherished and honoured is predominate. Solomon also knew this: *"Her children rise up and call her blessed; Her husband also, and he praises her"* (Proverbs 31:28).

A marriage can endure the multitude of adversities that life throws at it if we, as men, can just remember to love our wives at every turn along the way.

Some years ago, we attended a Gary Smalley marriage conference. As he was talking about this very same point, he pulled out a violin. I had no idea where he was going with the illustration as, like it does for most men, the violin evokes fear that some kind of sob story is coming. He then asked, "What if I told you this was a Stradivarius violin?" He then explained some of the history of Antonio Stradivarius, who lived in the seventeenth century and made history's most exquisite violins out of unique and exotic materials.[34] It was not clear to me if this was a true Stradivarius or not (I am guessing not), but when he began to pass it around, people handled it like it was the British Royal crown.

---

[34] There are only 650 Stradivarius violins remaining in the world and they are becoming almost priceless collector's items. The record price for sale at auction has been $15.9 million. Patricia Reaney, "Sale of Rare Stradivari Viola Could Set World Auction Record," *Reuters* (Thomson Reuters, March 27, 2014), https://www.reuters.com/article/us-auction-viola/sale-of-rare-stradivari-viola-could-set-world-auction-record-idUSBREA2Q19520140327.

After he observed the way that people carefully cradled and protected it as they passed it along, he took the opportunity to capture an inescapable point. "Men—that is how you need to treat your wives!" I will remember the illustration forever, although admittedly, the lesson sometimes still manages to escape me. It doesn't help that my little brain is full of unhelpful cultural idioms like, "I will play you like a cheap fiddle," which, of course, is clearly at odds with Smalley's valuable violin metaphor.

Our wives have an inherent God-given need to be loved and cherished. There are lots of men that know how to do this, to love their wives in word and in deed. "You look beautiful tonight," "What a great meal," "Nice job on the decorating," "I brought you flowers just because you are such a great wife every day." A marriage can endure the multitude of adversities that life throws at it if we, as men, can just remember to love our wives at every turn along the way.

Jack Benny was a radio and television personality who dominated the airwaves throughout the 1960s and 1970s. His on-air persona presented him as a penny-pinching cheapskate who would sooner die than part with a dollar. Yet in real life, his friends claimed he was generous and giving. Benny was married to his radio wife, Sayde Marks (better known as Mary Livingstone), for forty-eight years. Their marriage was far from idyllic. Benny was a typical philandering television star and Sayde was a sharp-tongued and demanding woman. After his death, Benny's widow joked that his signature gesture of holding one hand to the side of his face came about from his attempting to conceal scratch marks she'd inflicted on him after he had been caught with one of his female admirers.

Despite a tempestuous relationship, Jack loved his wife and was no stranger to showing his affection for her. One of the things Benny did was send Sayde a single red rose every day for the forty-eight years of their marriage. In 1974, the day after he passed away, a single red rose arrived at the door. She told the delivery service that Jack had passed away and they no longer needed to deliver the roses. The driver explained to her that Mr. Benny had made provision to keep the roses coming for the rest of her life. Sayde died in 1983 and the roses had kept coming until then. It was a simple act for a wealthy man, but that gesture alone may have gone a long way to ensuring that an otherwise tumultuous Hollywood marriage could last forty-eight years. Jack was far from being a perfect husband but there is no denying that he was passionate about his wife.

Two elderly couples got together one Saturday for an evening of playing cards. As the wives were in the kitchen making some tea, Joe confessed that his memory wasn't what it used to be and that he needed his wife's help remembering the cards. His friend Abe remarked that he used to have the same problem but was now attending a memory school where he was being taught to use word association to remember other things.

When Joe asked for the name of the memory school Abe said, "Ok, what's that red flower, it's very pretty, oh and it has thorns?"

Joe answered, "A rose?"

"Yeah… that's it, a rose!" Abe chimed, and turning towards the kitchen, he shouted, "Hey, Rose! What's the name of that memory school I'm going to?"

The other side of the equation is for wives to respect their husbands. Some men desire to hear words of love and to receive outward affection from their wives, but many need something else. Men, by and large, are ego driven. We want to achieve, succeed, and earn the respect of those around us. But there is one person on earth that we need respect from more than any other, and that is our wife.

We were once was at a pastors conference where Paul Yongi Cho was the keynote speaker. At the time, he was pastor of the world's largest church in Seoul, South Korea, with 700,000 members. (That is a church the size of the entire population of our city of Winnipeg.) Cho told a story about how, on Sunday afternoons after he had preached about six times, he would follow his wife around the house like a little puppy dog. Finally, she would turn to him and say, "What?" He would then ask her if she liked the morning's sermon. She would snap back at him, "You just had twenty thousand people tell you how good it was, so why do you want to hear it from me?" It was astounding to hear that this highly accomplished man, with all the awards and accolades in the world, needed expressed respect from his wife more than anything else in the world. I have told this story at pastor's conferences myself and will see ministers nodding their heads in agreement.

Paul apparently knew what he was talking about when he instructed wives to respect their husbands. Sadly, just as many husbands fail to understand the critical nature of showing their wives love, many wives struggle just the same in expressing respect for their husbands.

We are friends with a couple that we get together with from time to time, and the wife is outgoing and outspoken. She is fun-loving and always the life of the party, but I am always shocked when I hear her put down her husband in front of others. He pretends he doesn't care and that it is water off a duck's back, but I know that it cuts him deeply every time.

This might seem like merely a superficial and even selfish need for men to have but it is just the way God created them. Men are inherently warriors. We think that when we go off to work in the morning, we are really going off to storm the castle and slay the dragon. We just need the person most dear to us to notice and say, "Honey, thanks for slaying the dragon... and thanks for picking up milk on your way home from storming the castle. You're the best!"

One of the most inspiring stories you will ever hear is about a young couple named Mark and Susan. Mark was an Air Force officer and thirty-three-year-old Susan was a capable and independent woman with a career of her own. Due to a misdiagnosis and a horrible twist of fate, Susan was rendered completely blind.

Her new lot in life left her discouraged and in despair. Eventually, she knew she needed to get on with her life and go back to work. But how would she get there? She could no longer drive, and taking the bus, like she used to, seemed insurmountable.

Mark offered to drive her to work, even though it was entirely in the wrong direction from the Air Force base and would take him an hour out of his way each trip. After several weeks, Mark told Susan it just wasn't working and she would need to learn to take the bus.

At first, she reacted at the very notion. "I'm blind!" she responded bitterly. "How am I supposed to know where I'm going? I feel like you're abandoning me." Mark's heart broke to hear these words but he knew what had to be done.

After some consideration she realized that it was the right thing to do. Mark promised Susan that each morning and evening he would ride the bus with her, for as long as it took, until she got the hang of it. She could start counting the number of steps to cross the street and to enter her building and eventually she might become comfortable with it and be ready to tackle it on her own. For the next two weeks, Mark accompanied her to work, sitting beside her in his military uniform and helping her become accustomed to navigating the route safely to her office in total darkness.

Finally, Susan decided that she was ready to try the trip on her own. Monday morning arrived, and she managed without a hitch. And why wouldn't she? She had always been a capable person and that didn't need to change. As each day of the week came and went, her confidence was increasing. On Friday morning, Susan took the bus as usual. As she was exiting the bus, the driver said, "Boy, I sure envy you."

Susan wasn't sure if the driver was speaking to her or not. "Why do you say that you envy me, I'm a blind woman?"

The driver responded, "It must feel good to have someone who loves you so much."

Susan had no idea what the driver was talking about, and asked again, "What do you mean?"

The driver answered, "You know, every morning for the past week, a fine-looking gentleman in a military uniform has been standing across the corner watching you when you get off the bus. He makes sure you cross the street safely and he watches you until you enter your office building. Then he blows you a kiss, and gives you a little salute and walks away. You are one lucky lady."[35]

There is a lot to learn from this story, particularly for men. We can be real men, even ones that literally go off to fight the battle, and yet have the tenderness and care for our wives that they so deservedly need. Couples lie

---

[35] The original source of this story is unknown, but it has appeared in numerous writings, including: Jack Canfield, *Chicken Soup for the Couple's Soul: Inspirational Stories of Love and Relationships* (Deerfield Beach, FL: Health Communications, 1999).

to themselves when they claim that "there was never any real love in the marriage" or they "married the wrong person." If there was no love, why did they say I do? No, they got lost along the way somewhere and have forgotten that "it is not your love that will sustain your marriage, but your marriage that will sustain your love."

There is hope for every marriage that will decide to return to the love and respect that was designed into this relationship from the beginning of time. It is never easy, but it is never impossible either.

Chapter Eight

Ground Control to Major Tom

Tell my wife I love her very much she knows. Ground Control to Major Tom. Your circuit's dead, there's something wrong. Can you hear me, Major Tom?

—David Bowie

In 1969, David Bowie released the song "Space Oddity." It was the same year as the first moon landing, so it was auspicious timing.

Esoteric songs like this are always a bit hard to understand and "Space Oddity" is even more difficult, given the fact that Bowie was a serious drug addict when he wrote the song. Who really knows what he meant? He once said he didn't even really remember. But I have my own interpretation. As Major Tom cuts off transmission with earth and drifts aimlessly into space, the last thing he says is, "Tell my wife I love her very much—she knows." Major Tom is the typical emotionally detached male. He knows that his wife knows that he loves her but he has a hard time actually telling her.

Kathy asked me just the other day why I don't tell her every day I love her like some husbands do. I told her, "Look, I told you on our wedding night, and if it changes I will let you know." *ba-dum-tsh* (rimshot)

Even though the Apostle Paul boils marriage down to two responses, love and respect, that might be an oversimplification. If you have read extensively on the subject of marriage, you can easily get a bit overwhelmed by the multitude of voices on the subject. The way to avoid the complexity of it all is to boil it down to the Four Big Cs of a successful marriage. They are: Communication, Common Interests, Consideration and Christ.

1. COMMUNICATION

Any time you witness a truly passionate, successful marriage, you will undoubtedly see communication, common interests, consideration and Christ. These Four Big Cs rank far above the sexual passions that usually get all the press from Hollywood. None of them are more important than communication. And when it comes to communication, there is a big difference between listening and hearing. Men are far better at hearing than listening.

Communication is far and away the single greatest key to any successful relationship. In marriage, it is the needle and thread that sews two separate lives together into one.

One evening I was watching *American Ninja Warrior*. This is not light-duty mindless television, as you have to pay close attention—a contestant could fall off an obstacle at any time and you do not want to have to wait for the instant replay to see what happened. While I was watching, Kathy came into the room and said, "Good, you're not doing anything. I want to talk to you about something." Why she thought I was not doing anything was beyond me.

So, she continued on. I could hear her but I wasn't actually listening. Then, out of the corner of my ear (if ears have corners), I heard her ask, "So, what do you think?"

Now I was hooped. If I admitted I wasn't actually listening and asked her to repeat the question, she was going to be mad. I decided it was better to just pretend I was listening, so I tentatively answered, "Sure... that sounds good." I was a little nervous when I saw how excited she was about my answer, but it was out there now, and soon enough I would discover what I had agreed to. *What's the worst that could happen?* I thought.

The next week we attended our first ballroom dancing class. I am not joking, I literally agreed to take up ballroom dancing because I could not pull myself away from the television set! Nevertheless, it only lasted twenty-six weeks and I just pretended I was in the preliminary rounds of *American Ninja Warrior* and showed up every Friday night with the intention of dominating the field. It ended up being a lot of fun and did wonders for our marriage, as we now had a built-in weekly date night. On an off night when we weren't "winning," I just reminded myself it could have been worse. Much worse!

Anna and Loren Bronkhorst were spending a quiet evening together watching television like many couples do in their designated easy chairs. Loren decided to retire for the night and headed to bed. The next night, he joined Anna again in front of the TV and again headed to bed before her. It was not until the third day that Loren realized that the reason Anna was staying up so late was that she had been dead for three days and he hadn't even noticed.[36]

Husbands and wives often approach the concept of communication quite differently. For instance, a wife will think, "Our marriage is in trouble; we had better talk." A husband will think, "Our marriage is in trouble; I had better keep my mouth shut."

Communication is far and away the single greatest key to any successful relationship. In marriage, it is the needle and thread that sews two separate lives together into one. Take communication out of the equation and you will find two people desperately floundering to make any sense of this life sentence we call marriage.

It is surprising how long a marriage can last without any semblance of meaningful dialogue. The modern family is now so immensely busy with careers, hobbies, sports, children, school events, kids' sports, financial worries and extended family commitments that the lack of relational intimacy can go largely ignored until it reaches the breaking point—and it eventually will. That day usually comes when the kids have become independent or have gone off to college and the couple looks across the dinner table and thinks, "Who are you?" More often than not, in the absence of dramatic action, this couple is headed for separation. The years found a way to drift by unnoticed and the hapless couple are just two ships passing

---

[36]   I've been telling this story for so long that I do not remember where I first read it. I am pretty sure I would not have made up a name like Bronkhorst, so it must be true.

in the night, typically, on their way to the bathroom. They are little more than cohabiting adults without the benefit of meaningful conversation. They were busy enough, but they did not invest enough time into their own personal relationship to sustain them past the child-raising season.

We have seen this countless times. It is profoundly sad, as they are now heading into the years where they might finally have some time and money to enjoy life together, but instead, they find themselves alone in their later years. Of course, many times they just move on and find someone else. The church is full of couples like this, and we embrace them and love them and try to help them succeed in round two. We are happy for them when they are able to get it right the second time. But it just feels like they may have missed God's best, which Solomon called "rejoicing in the wife of your youth."

Regardless of where we may be on the journey, it is never too late to establish the relational foundation of meaningful conversation. There are at least five distinct levels of communication in marriage.[37] They are: small talk, self-talk, serious talk, sweet talk and soul talk. Each one has the potential to take a relationship to the next deeper level.

Small Talk

Small talk is entry-level communication about "whatever." It is not about anything particularly important. You can make small talk in the grocery store with a complete stranger. "How about them Jets?" There is nothing wrong with small talk; it opens up a conduit for further, more meaningful conversation and primes the pump to move a relationship to a deeper level.

Couples engage in small talk every day: "Looks like rain." "Yup, looks like rain, better take an umbrella." When people say they are not good at small talk, chances are they are not good at any kind of talk. Because married couples spend so much time together, they will end up talking about anything and everything during the course of a day. Kathy will describe

---

[37] Scott Bayles, *The Greatest Commands: Learning How to Love Like Jesus*, (Scott Bayles, 2008), p. 50. Pastor Robert J. Morgan sometimes gets credit for identifying the five distinct levels of communication, but I have seen it elsewhere as well.

recipes in great detail to me and I will tell her about the metallurgical properties of her frying pan. Neither of us really cares about the other thing.

Nobody, and I mean nobody, wants to spend all day, every day discussing their deepest emotional turmoil. There is a place for all levels of communication. Without the benefit of small talk you could die in front of the TV and your spouse might not even notice.

Self-Talk

Self-talk is when we talk about ourselves—our health, our hobbies, our headaches. It is not necessarily conversation on a deep level but it does begin to draw things to a personal level.

Men are particularly good at self-talk because they are talking about their favorite subject, themselves. It's like the woman at her fiftieth anniversary who was asked what the secret to marriage longevity was. Without missing a beat, she said, "I guess it has worked because for all these years we have both been in love with the same man." I suppose it would be funnier if it were not true.

We had a friend who worked for the Federal government investigating tax fraud. She was very good at her job because she understood the male mindset. She told us that all she had to do was take a genuine interest in what it was that he actually did for a living, and he could not help himself and would end up spilling the beans on whatever it was that he was up to.

Men (and women) love to talk about themselves and their interests. It is perplexing how many women will complain that their husbands don't talk. They will; you just have to take an interest in the subjects that they love to talk about. A wife that has what she considers a "non-communicating" husband will do well by merely taking an interest in his particular passions. It might be motorcycles, ice hockey, politics or *American Ninja Warrior*, but at least she will get him talking and that light duty conversation might be just the thing that leads to the meaningful conversation she craves.

We have a grown son who is much quieter than his father. If the subject is not of particular interest to him, he will be content to listen, smile, laugh occasionally or throw in the odd witty comment. Or, he might just tune out and start doing something on his phone. But, getting him to open up is the easiest thing in the world. Just ask him about the world of technology or business or world travel or sports, which are his areas of passion, and he will talk non-stop all night.

Self-talk is an essential part of any relationship and an indispensable part of any marriage.

SERIOUS TALK

Serious talk is when the conversation takes a dramatic turn towards the serious issues of life: finances and bills, legal issues, child raising, little Johnny's problems at school and any of the things that families have to wrestle with. You do not engage in serious talk with strangers, or at least you shouldn't. It's none of their business, but it is the business of your spouse.

It is surprising how many couples struggle with this and allow serious unresolved issues to fester.

Money problems are one of the biggest relationship killers in marriage. However, it is not the money per se that is the problem but the communication, or lack thereof, around money. It is the questions about saving versus spending, the priorities of spending, borrowing, and the stresses of debt that produce the conflict. The biggest problem is the failure to talk about it at all. A family can be struggling with crippling debt and the wife might come home with a brand new dress without having had any prior discussion about it with her husband. Rather than leading to serious talk, it precipitates a full blown, five-alarm shouting match. Now, a man would never do this! By this I mean bring home a new dress. He would be more likely to show up with a new motorcycle. Go big or go home! You know, boys and their toys! It really doesn't matter whether a couple has money or not, every marriage will struggle at some point in their communication over money.

A group of men were in the locker room at the country club after their golf game. A cell phone rings on the changeroom bench and a man picks up. The others cannot help but listen in.

The woman on the other end says, "Are you at the club?"

The man confirms, "Yes."

She continues, "I'm at mall and that fur coat I love is for sale for one thousand dollars. Should I get it?"

"Well, if you really like it, I don't see why not," he responds.

"And, oh, I dropped by the Mercedes dealer this morning and they have the new SL550 on the lot for $100,000. It's the only one they are going to be getting in red. What do you think?"

"What do I think?" he responds, "I think at that price you would be crazy to pass up."

Finally, she says, "Oh, and the real estate agent called and the price on the house we are looking at has been reduced from $2.1 million to only $1.8 million… should we pull the trigger?"

"Hey, why not?" he says, "You only live once."

At that he hung up and turned to his fellow golfers and asked, "Anybody know whose phone this is? His wife is totally out of control!"

There are just too many serious issues in marriage to ignore them. And there are very few that cannot be resolved by just talking them through.

Sweet Talk

Sweet talk is just what it sounds like, those cutesy things that couples say to each other as terms of endearment. It is when we express the personal affection we have for each other with our words. If a marriage cannot get to this point of endearing talk, it will have a hard time surviving rough patches along the way.

Many couples have developed nicknames like "Sweetie," or "Sweetheart," or "Schnookums," or "Are you SERIOUS?" Normally, these are things reserved only for those with whom we are truly intimate, unless, of course, you live in the South. We were driving through Alabama one time and we stopped for gas. The female clerk, who was half my age, called me "Honey" twice, "Hon" three times and "Sweetheart" another three times. When I got back in the car, I told Kathy I was worried I might be having an affair with the gal inside but I wasn't entirely sure.

In Larry King's last CNN interview with Billy Graham in 2005, Larry asked him about his marriage of sixty-one years to Ruth. Billy Graham said these touching things:

Her health is not very good. She's an invalid... Well, I'd like to see us hold hands and go together because I love her so much. And I love her more now—interestingly, I love her more now, and we have more romance now than we did when we were young. We both agree to that, and... We don't have the physical love, but we have eye contact that tells you I love you and there is not a single day, not a single night after "Larry King" that I don't say "I love you" and I love her with all my heart."[38]

Many young people would have a hard time believing that a ninety-year-old couple would be more in love than when they were younger, but I have witnessed it hundreds of times in ministry and would say the same thing with regard to my almost forty years with Kathy.

People say that marriage is like a fine wine that gets better with age. I would have no idea, as I never drink the stuff and would prefer a strawberry milkshake any day, which seems like a better analogy for sweet talk anyway.

Soul Talk

The highest level we can get to in conversation is soul talk. This is where we open up about our deepest thoughts, dreams, fears and insecurities. Not surprisingly, it is not uncommon for men to struggle with soul talk. They would rather talk about fuel injectors or fishing lures any day of the week. Their wives will pine on hopelessly, "I just want to know what he's thinking!" I'll tell you what he's thinking: NOTHING! What makes you think he's thinking about anything?

Humorist Dave Barry puts it this way;

A guy in a relationship is like an ant standing on top of a truck tire. The ant is aware, on a very basic level, that something large is there, but he cannot even dimly comprehend what this thing is, or the nature of his involvement with it. And if the truck starts moving, and the tire starts to roll, the ant will sense that something important is happening,

---

38 "Interview with Billy Graham," *Larry King Live* (CNN, June 16, 2005), Retrieved June 4, 2020, from http://transcripts.cnn.com/TRANSCRIPTS/0506/16/lkl.01.html.

but right up until he rolls around to the bottom and is squashed into a small black blot, the only distinct thought that will form in his tiny brain will be, and I quote, "Huh!"[39]

Notwithstanding the male struggle with emotional intimacy, men have as much need as woman to engage in this level of soul talk. However, you cannot and should not go there with too many people in this world. There needs to be a level of trust that can endure this kind of transparency. There are people who have a few close friends that they can share with at this level, but if their spouse is not one of them, then that marriage may be headed for trouble.

When we communicate at this level, we often end up producing an emotional bond. This is why soul talk is generally inappropriate with a member of the opposite sex that is not our spouse. Very few adulterous affairs start with sex. They start with seemingly innocent conversations that transgress the level of intimacy that one should reserve for someone who is your spouse. Psychologists have concluded that this kind of emotional intimacy promotes the possibility of sexual intimacy in the future.[40]

In pastoral ministry we see this pattern repeated again and again by people who did not think they were doing anything wrong until it was too late. I have seen pastors themselves get too emotionally invested while counselling a member of the opposite sex. As she is pouring out her heart to her pastor, a female congregant starts to think, "Wow, Pastor Bob is sensitive and caring and really understands what I am going through." The next thing you know there are misplaced affections on both sides of the desk. (I protect myself from these situations by being sort of a jerk so nobody wants to come back and see me again. Works like a charm.)

Everybody needs soul talk, and if we don't find it in the right place we may look in the wrong place. With the advent of the internet, this kind of emotional infidelity is almost epidemic. When we see a marriage that

---

[39] Dave Barry, *Dave Barry's Complete Guide to Guys* (New York: Ballantine Books, 1995), p. 83.

[40] Seth Meyers, "How to Define Emotional Infidelity: Types of Cheating," *Psychology Today* (Sussex Publishers, June 22, 2011), https://www.psychologytoday.com/blog/insight-is-2020/201106/how-define-emotional-infidelity-different-types-cheating.

is heading for rocky shores like a ship without a rudder, that couple has almost always lost contact emotionally with each other. In the immortal words of Cool Hand Luke, "What we have here is a failure to communicate."[41] If you remember the movie starring Paul Newman, those were Lucas Jackson's famous last words… just before they shot him dead. Those words are infamous relationship killers too.

In the book of Genesis, God creates Adam and Eve and places them in the garden. It says they were naked and unashamed. One can only assume that they had no secrets, since they had nothing to hide and nowhere to hide it. Eve was the first woman who could go to her closet and honestly say, "I don't have a thing to wear." By chapter three, Eve gets tempted and the two of them are chowing down on forbidden fruit. It says, "Then the eyes of both of them were opened, and they knew that they were naked…" (3:7). God comes looking for them and Adam hides in the bushes, *"Where are you?"* (3:9). Look carefully at Adam's next words, *"I heard Your voice in the garden, and I was afraid because I was naked; and I hid myself"* (3:10).

When sin came into Adam's life, he became ashamed and insecure because of his nakedness. His intimate relationships with God and with Eve were broken. It is no different today; we struggle in our relationships because we are insecure in our vulnerabilities, even with our spouse.

Marriage is the proper domain for soul talk. Being able to open up about everything going on inside draws a couple together and produces a desire to help the other person accomplish their dreams or overcome their fears. Deep down, we all want to know and be known by the people closest to us.

Even after a long drought in a superficial relationship, all it takes is one party to open up and start the journey afresh. Passionate couples care deeply about what is in the other person's heart, and these kinds of marriages can survive any adversity that this world throws at them.

---

41   *Cool Hand Luke,* dir. Stuart Rosenberg, United States: Warner Bros., 1967.

Chapter Nine

The Common Bond

Men have nothing in common with me—there is no point of contact; they have foolish little feelings and foolish little vanities and impertinences and ambitions; their foolish little life is but a laugh, a sigh, and extinction.
— Mark Twain, *The Mysterious Stranger*

We have lived in the same house for thirty years. It is a well-constructed home that was built by a geo-scientist. However, he was more concerned with strength than beauty. The second floor has lovely cedar siding, but the main floor came with a front veneer of bare concrete blocks that looked like the outside of a prison. We bought the house knowing that someday we could fix up the esthetics.

Finally, after living in the eyesore for far too long, I purchased some spectacular manmade dry-stack rocks that would look great against the cedar. When the bricklayer arrived, he advised us that his price for labour was going to be only $2,400 and that he could be done in a day and a half.

He should not have told me that last piece of information. When I did the math in my head, I realized he was charging me two hundred dollars an hour. I sarcastically asked him what law school he had attended. When he gave me a not-unexpected confused look, I explained to him that at that hourly rate he must be a lawyer.

Now that we had both successfully offended one another, he went on his way. Serendipitously, that very afternoon I was looking for something in my basement workshop and found some strange tools that I did not know I had. It was an entire box of bricklaying tools: trowels, hawks and the like. I figured if I owned the tools, then I must somehow know how to lay bricks. After a quick YouTube review, I concluded, "How hard could it be?"

That afternoon, I was in the front of the house laying brick. I was overcome by this strange feeling that I had been doing it all my life and I was laying in those rocks like a pro. Aldo, my Italian neighbour, walked over and asked me how I knew how to lay bricks. I simply reminded him of my Italian heritage. It is a little-known fact that all Italians know how to lay tile and brick. It is like the old joke: "How do you break up an Italian wedding? Just shout, 'The tile is here!'" I finished the wall in a day and a half, saved $2,400 and earned some serious new bragging rights. And maybe, somewhat surprisingly, the wall is still standing proud today and looks just fine.

One of the most important techniques in bricklaying is what is called the "common bond." Every five or six courses, they will use a row of bricks that run *between* the inner wall and the outer wall to hold the two walls together. Loadbearing walls need to be constructed this way, as a single brick wall would just buckle under the weight. We have all seen these walls thousands of times, but unless we knew what we were looking for we would never have noticed. It is hard to describe in words what it looks like, but suffice it to say, it is exactly what the name denotes—bricks that are common to both walls and prevent them from separating and collapsing, which they most certainly will without the *common bond*. Which brings me to the second Big C: Common Interests.

2. Common Interests

A couple will not and should not have everything in common—nobody wants to marry themselves.

One of the biggest determining factors in a successful marriage is the common bond, or what most people would refer to as common interests. These are the things in couples' lives that they share in common: hobbies, sports, pastimes, travel, fitness, art, food, values, and of course, faith.

Clinical psychologist and founder of the eHarmony internet dating service, Neil Clark Warren, says this:

> The healthiest and most successful marriages I've ever witnessed were between people who had a high level of similarity BEFORE they were married.[42]

Specifically, he elaborates,

> If the two of you can have about five interests in common, and if those interests span several categories, I promise you that it will tend to pull you together. It will tend to weave your lives into one whole. It will benefit your marriage all the years of your life.[43]

A couple will not and should not have everything in common—nobody wants to marry themselves. Just ask Jerry Seinfeld about when he was engaged to Jeannie Steinman (played by Janeane Garofalo) in season eight of his iconic television series. She was presented as a female version of Jerry. She made witty sarcastic cracks and ate breakfast cereal for every meal, just like him. At first, they thought it was a dream come true. Then the two realized they could not stand each other and broke off the engagement at the coffee shop, simultaneously saying, "I hate you!"[44]

Nevertheless, any marriage needs enough things in common to hold the relationship together. Dr. Warren says five or six are all it takes. However, the more things in common, the stronger the common bond.

When our grown children were in the season of finding life mates, we coached them about this. We reminded them that what they were ultimately looking for was a life partner, someone with whom to do life

---

42 Neil Clark Warren and eHarmony Research Library, "Common Interests, Values and Other Crucial Similarities," Crosswalk.com (Salem Media Group, March 10, 2003), https://www.crosswalk.com/family/singles/common-interests-values-and-other-crucial-similarities-1185584.html.

43 Ibid.

44 "The Foundation," *Seinfeld episode 8, no. 1*, written by Alec Berg and Jeff Schaffer, directed by Andy Ackerman, September 19, 1996.

together for a very long time. They might be drawn to a very attractive person, but without sharing a common faith, common values and common interests, that marriage would require a lot more work and probably less fun just to keep it together.

The old adage that "opposites attract" might be true about magnets, but it produces a multiple of challenges in marriage—he wants to go golfing, she wants to go shopping; he wants to go out for pizza, she wants sushi; he wants to go to the mountains skiing on vacation, she wants to go to a warm beach. If there are too many of these disparities, then when and how does the couple connect recreationally?

Kathy and I have lots of things we don't share in common, like spitting, sarcasm, scuba diving, sauerkraut, mustard, kale, *American Ninja Warrior*, *Dancing with the Stars*, eighties rock and Adele… you can probably figure out who likes what. Couples need their own space, their own interests and their own friends as well. But one of the reasons our marriage has thrived going on forty years is that we do so many things together.

Shared interests do not magically appear just because you love one another. You have to work at discovering which things, when done together with another person rather than individually, could become activities that you both love.

When we first met, I had one singular compelling, possibly obsessive, passion, and that was snow skiing. I once skied 110 days in a single season. That basically meant I did not do anything else, like work, for months on end. Kathy realized early on that it might be the right move to take up skiing so that she did not become a winter widow. The first ski trip we went on, I stuck her in lessons for the entire week and skied by myself. Yes, she married a real caveman. It didn't take long for her to move through the levels and today she can keep up with me on any slope. She still doesn't sit around all summer waiting for snow, but she genuinely enjoys the sport and we love travelling to different ski areas to explore God's creation. I know it doesn't seem fair that one person has to come over to another's interests, but it is fascinating how you can learn to enjoy just about anything. Have I mentioned my love for ballroom dancing?

There are some fortunate couples that have much in common right from the get-go; they love the same food, same movies, same sports, same vacation spots and even the same church. These couples are more the exception than the rule.

Most marriages start with a few common interests and need to build upon them from there. Some are in the unenviable position of having few common binds, and they need to put in a real effort to make it work. You would be surprised at how many couples today do not even attend the same church.

Manuel and Anita have had a difficult married life. They share a common ethnic heritage and two children, whom they both love dearly, but they did not have a lot of other commonalities. Their marriage has banged up on the rocks many times, and to their credit, they continued to try to make it work. If you were to ask Anita if there was one thing that saved their marriage, she would tell you it was hockey. Yes, hockey! Not playing it—watching it. Their son won a hockey scholarship and was playing at a college level. Travelling to games and watching him play became the glue that drew them together. Anita grew quite versed in the game and could talk strategy and technique. Their daughter tagged along and was a good sport about it as well. The most important thing was that it was something they were able to do together, even though they started a mile apart in their interests. They had to make some choices to make it happen, but they did. Not many wives can say, "Hockey saved our marriage."

3. Consideration

The third Big C in a successful marriage is Consideration. It is profoundly simple, immeasurably powerful and strangely elusive. A husband was asked by a marriage counsellor if his wife was hard to please. Bewildered, he answered, "I don't know; I have never tried."

Philippians 2:4–5 says, *"Let each of you look out not only for his own interests, but also for the interests of others. Let this mind be in you which was also in Christ Jesus..."* Jesus' nature was always to put other people's needs ahead of His own. This was not just witnessed in His work on the cross but also in how He conducted Himself every day on earth. He would spend all day ministering to people and then try to escape for a few private moments at the end of the day, and the crowd would selfishly follow Him. Rather than being annoyed, He showed them even more compassion. *"And when Jesus went out He saw a great multitude; and He was moved with compassion for them, and healed their sick"* (Matthew 14:14).

It is always safe to go with the "What would Jesus do?" approach, but when it comes to marriage there is far more here than meets the eye. The most significant metaphor used in Scripture to describe Jesus and His church is that of a bride and a bridegroom. We sometimes make a lot of the fact that Jesus was single while on earth, but that may have been only because he was preparing for the greatest marital union of all time— between Himself and the church. In Ephesians 5, Paul gives some insightful instructions about making a marriage work, and then, out of nowhere, says he is actually talking about Christ and His bride, the church: *"This is a great mystery, but I speak concerning Christ and the church"* (5:32). He is, in fact, still talking about marriage, but he is employing a spiritual analogy to explain how husbands should treat their wives. (In theology this is sometimes called The Law of Double Reference, when both earthly and heavenly things are spoken of at the same time.)

Here is Paul's big idea on marriage:

Therefore, just as the church is subject to Christ, so let the wives be to their own husbands in everything. Husbands, love your wives, just as Christ also loved the church and gave Himself for her.

—Ephesians 5:24–25

The modern woman may bristle at the idea of being subject to her husband in everything, but there is a bigger picture here to discover. Paul tells husbands to love their wives as Christ loved the church. How did Christ love the church? He put our needs far ahead of His own and was willing to die for us. The way a husband is to love his wife is to put her needs ahead of his own. If a wife knew that her husband always had her best interests in mind in every situation, she would gladly grant her husband leadership in their relationship.

It is to be a symbiotic relationship. He doesn't *take* authority in the relationship, she *offers* it. It all breaks down as soon a husband starts to demand submission from his wife, or vice versa.

Again, look at it in terms of Christ and the church. How much authority does He have over us? In theory, one hundred percent, but in practice, only what we give Him. For example, He has authority over all our finances. Yet, in practice He only gets what we are willing to give him.

Authority (let's just call it leadership so it does not sound so imposing) is based on submission. We only have as much leadership as people give us through their submission. This goes for a sports coach, a company manager, a husband, a wife or a parent. What Paul has described here as love and submission is in fact nothing more than mutual consideration—putting the needs of the other person ahead of your own.

> *Yes, all of you be submissive to one another, and be clothed with humility, for "God resists the proud, But gives grace to the humble."*
>
> —1 Peter 5:5

The Toilet Seat Theory

Dr. John Gottman stands alone as the world's foremost expert on couples therapy.[45] As a researcher for the University of Washington Department of Psychology, he has studied thousands of couples over periods of multiple years and has emerged with some incredibly important findings. It is claimed that he can predict, with over ninety percent accuracy, if a couple's marriage will end in divorce.[46]

His research began in earnest in 1986 when he set up The Love Lab. He brought newlywed couples into the lab and watched them interact with each other. His team of researchers hooked the couples up to electrodes and

---

[45] Katy Butler, "The Gottman Method: Couples Therapy Under the Microscope," Psychotherapy Networker, accessed July 20, 2020, https://www.psychotherapynetworker.org/blog/details/430/the-gottman-method-couples-therapy-under-the-microscope.

[46] Ibid.

asked them to speak about their relationship… things like how they met, conflicts, positive and negative memories, etc. As they spoke, the electrodes measured the subjects' blood flow, heart rates and body sweat. There was nothing Dr. Strangelove about it. The couples were then sent home and asked to come back in six years to see if they were still together.[47]

Gottman compiled the data and separated the couples into two groups: *the masters* and *the disasters*. The masters were still happily married after six years. The disasters had either broken up or were chronically unhappy. The distinguishing factors between the two groups had little to do with their actual answers but with the levels of stress going on in the inside as measured by their vital signs, such as their higher heart rates, blood flow and sweat gland activity. Simply put, Gottman found that the more physiologically active the couples were in the lab, the quicker their relationships deteriorated over time.

Whether a man puts the toilet seat down holds a major clue to the success of a marriage; it is a sign that he understands and respects his wife's needs.

Dr. Gottman then took the research to the next level and followed 670 couples of all ages for up to twenty-five years. He looked for the common factors that led to either marital success or failure. His research showed that the single most important factor that determined marital success was whether a couple can continually show one another kindness and consideration in daily life. "Contrary to popular belief," says Gottman, "it is the mundane events of everyday life that build love in marriage. Connecting in the countless 'mindless moments' that usually go by unnoticed establishes a positive emotional climate."[48]

---

[47] Emily Esfahani Smith, "The Secret to Love Is Just Kindness," *The Atlantic* (Atlantic Media Company, May 11, 2020), https://www.theatlantic.com/health/archive/2014/06/happily-ever-after/372573/.

[48] Hara Estroff Marano, "Rescuing Marriages Before They Begin," Smart Marriages® (CMFCE, LLC, May 28, 1997), http://www.smartmarriages.com/marano.html.

His thesis has now become known as The Toilet Seat Theory.[49] Whether a man puts the toilet seat down holds a major clue to the success of a marriage; it is a sign that he understands and respects his wife's needs and is open to the kind of giving and taking of influence that leads to long-term marital stability. Gottman's research revealed that only twenty percent of divorces are caused by an affair. He concludes, "Most marriages die with a whimper, as people turn away from one another, slowly growing apart."[50]

We were watching an old episode of *Shark Tank* on CNBC, which is basically the "all *Shark Tank,* all the time" station. A young couple, Nicholas and Alessia Galekovic, founders of Beard King, came on pitching a kitschy product called the Beard Bib. It is a plastic bib that attaches to the bathroom mirror to catch the hair when a man trims his beard. None of the Sharks offered up a deal, but unwilling to walk away from the table, this savvy couple pitched Lori Greiner a deal for a whopping forty-five percent stake of the company for $100,000.

Knowing the show had been taped months earlier, I looked up the story online to find out what had happened since it aired. In the end, they never closed on the deal with Lori—they didn't need to, because sales jumped four hundred percent the day the episode aired and the company grew from $140,000, to $700,000 to $1.6 million in the next two years.

The wife, Alessia, emerged as the real salesperson when she said that it was women who are buying this product because they can't stand the mess their men leave when they trim their beards. Even if men now all want to grow hipster beards and look like cavemen, it does not mean their wives want them acting like one. All that is required to keep a marriage solvent is a tiny bit of consideration for one another.

A couple was struggling desperately in their marriage and finally agreed to see a marriage counsellor. After listening to fifty minutes of the wife complaining bitterly about the faults of her husband, the counsellor walked across the room and planted a huge, moist kiss on her lips. This brought her to deaf silence. He then turned to her husband and said, "All she needs is one of those twice a week and all your problems are over."

---

49   Ibid.

50   Ibid.

Genuinely impressed, the husband said, "Perfect. I can bring her by Tuesdays and Thursdays."

4. Christ

The fourth and final Big C is Christ. It might seem a bit cliché to say you just need Jesus, but it is a mystery to me how any marriage can stay together without the foundation of Christ. There are just too may forces conspiring against its survival.

Several years ago, we were over at the home of a young couple with children. Their marriage was in crisis: they were not communicating, had few common interests and were lacking in even rudimentary consideration for each other. To make matters worse, they had dropped out of church and were receiving nothing in the way of life-giving teaching or encouragement from other believers. After listening to a long litany of complaints, I bluntly explained that if they did not return Christ to the centre of their relationship they had no hope for a future together. The genius of a Christ-centred marriage is that as we draw closer to Him, we will, by necessity, draw closer together. It is mere physics.

In an attempt to bolster my argument, Kathy said this, "It's really true. If we didn't have Jesus in our life, I would have left Mark a long time ago."

Somewhat stunned by the comment, I didn't say anything about it in the moment. But on the way home in the car, I brought it up.

"What do you mean you would have left me a long time ago if we didn't have Christ in our marriage?"

She casually explained, "I was just trying to be empathetic that I understood what she was going through."

Still in somewhat of a state of confusion I responded, "Ok, but was it necessary to be quite so self-disclosing?"

Still dropping the plow in a little deeper, she elaborated, "Well, you're not the easiest person to live with!"

At that, I decided to drop it before we had to call someone to come counsel us! Today we have a good laugh about her overly-honest counselling moment, and because we do have Christ in our life we are still married and still in love. Unfortunately, that couple's marriage sadly ended up in divorce. Edward Mote's great hymn says it all: *"On Christ, the solid Rock, I stand; All other ground is sinking sand."*

Here is a far more redemptive story. Henry was a hard-living, tough-talking truck driver. As a result of his long hauls on the road, he was physically and emotionally detached from his wife, Debby. She came to our church most every week and we rarely, if ever, saw him, as he was not a Christian and had no need for such a "crutch." While he was off trucking for days on end, she began to quite innocently frequent online chatrooms. It did not take long before she connected with someone that finally "got her." An emotional connection began and eventually she decided to leave Henry and go to Florida and move in with this man whom she had never even met in person. Debby followed through with her plan and divorced Henry, even though they had been married thirty years and had grown children. It was the type of tragic story that is all too common.

About a year later, God, in His sovereignty, decided to pay Henry a visit while he was trucking down the road. An overwhelming sense came over him as to what a poor husband he had been for his entire married life. He began to sob uncontrollably, a man who had never cried in his adult life. He had tears flowing at such a rate he could no longer see the road. He pulled his big rig semi off to the side of the road and, right then and there, he gave his life to Christ.

Meanwhile, down in Florida, God was working on Debby at the same time. She had no idea that Henry had just given his life to Christ, but she had become overwhelmed with her own sense of sin and impropriety. She decided she was going to leave Mr. Palm Beach and implore her husband Henry to forgive her and take her back. When she called, she discovered a new Henry, a broken and contrite man full of a willingness to forgive.

After her return to Winnipeg, the couple came to see me one Monday and told me this remarkable story. They wanted to know if I would consider remarrying them. I told them the soonest I could do it was Tuesday, but only because they needed twenty-four hours for a marriage license to take effect. The next day they stood in my office and recommitted their marital vows. Every Sunday, Henry and Debby walk into the church holding hands and sit together as a testimony of God's great grace.

I don't think I will ever get over the sense of awe at just how great our God is. Nothing is impossible for Him.

Chapter Ten

Fifty Shades of Black

Sex is the consolation you have when you can't have love.
—Gabriel García Márquez

I have never seen the movie or read the book *Fifty Shades of Grey*. Probably nobody should. Somehow, the knowledge that it was written by a married woman and mother of two seemed to mitigate the fact that it was misogynistic pornography. One hundred million people, mostly women, read the book. What I do know about the story is that it is the tale of an older, rich and handsome man leading a much younger virginal woman into a dark world of bondage and sadomasochistic sex.

In an era of rampant sexual abuse, violence against women and epidemic human trafficking for the sex trade, I don't know why anyone could call this art—except for the fact that our world has become hyper-sexualized and has lost all perspective of normal human sexuality. And trashy novels are nothing new to women's literature. The sweeping generalization is that men like to watch pornography and women like to read about it.

For the record, this is not an anti-sex, puritanical rant. Sex is good. Sex is fun. Sex is even holy. Sex was God's idea, and in fact, it was His very first command to man. He created Adam and Eve, placed them naked in the Garden of Eden and said, "Be fruitful and multiply…" (Genesis 1:28), and in case we didn't catch the euphemism, any ambiguity is cleared up for us later when we read, "Now Adam knew Eve his wife, and she conceived and bore Cain…"(Genesis 4:1). So, in other words, God commanded them to have sex and they willfully obeyed. It was one of the easier commandments to keep.

The irony of the male lead's name, Christian Grey, in *Fifty Shades of Grey* should not be lost on us. Although she has never admitted it, author E. L. James likely chose the name as a backhanded swipe at Christian moral piety. Sadly, it may actually be fitting, as modern Christians have fallen headlong into the greyed world of confused sexuality. From God's perspective there are no shades of grey, only black and white.

The life of Abraham's grandson, Jacob, is a good example (or a bad one, depending on how you look at it). He ended up with four wives and is a case study on how *not* to be happily married. He made a deal with his Uncle Laban to work for seven years for his daughter Rachel's hand in marriage. On the wedding day, Laban pulled the old switcheroo and pawned off the older, shall we say, less attractive daughter, Leah, on the sexually pent-up Jacob. The wedding night must have been agreeable, since Jacob didn't even notice he had the wrong girl until the next morning. Undaunted, he then made another deal with Laban to get the younger, more attractive daughter, Rachel, as his next wife—after another seven-year work contract. And Jacob was supposed to be the shrewd one?

Strangely, I can personally relate to the story of Jacob more than most. When I went on my very first date with my now wife, Kathy, her father met me at the door. He was dismayed that I wanted to take out his youngest daughter, who was a full four years younger than I was.

Leering at me, he said, "Are you sure you are not looking for Patty? She's the one your age."

To which, in my incurable smart-alecky way, I said, "Sure. I'm fine with either one."

That did not endear me to him, and I had to work at the son-in-law relationship for seven years until he warmed up to me. And catch this, his name was Laban. (Okay that part isn't true. But I can't read the story of Jacob without thinking of my own journey and how grateful I am that I only married one of them.)

So off Jacob went with his two wives, finally leaving behind the manipulative world of Uncle Laban. However, being a somewhat typical male of high sexual drive and low self-control, he slept with his wives' handmaidens and "voila"—two more wives! Within Jacob's little collection of four wives there was no shortage of bitterness and jealousy. We have no record of how Solomon's massive harem got along, but one can only imagine it was a nest of envy and strife.

This raises an important question. Why did he have to marry all four women? Simply put, there were no wedding ceremonies in those earliest days; if you slept with a woman, that made her your wife. This, in itself, was the main reason for multiple marriages in the Old Testament. If we had the same rule today, and if we can believe Wilt Chamberlain's locker room tales, he would have twenty thousand wives, making Solomon look like a novice.[51] Even in the New Testament, the Apostle Paul cryptically makes reference to the sex-equals-marriage notion. I know that when most of us read this verse we are somewhat bewildered as to the meaning.

Or do you not know that he who is joined to a harlot is one body with her? For "the two," He says, "shall become one flesh."

—1 Corinthians 6:16

When I was in my early twenties, I had become a Christian while most of my friends had not. These guys were out sowing their wild oats, as is the way young men conduct themselves today as well. One of my friends, Mick, was always going on about his girl problems. He would tell me how clingy and possessive they would become and how he didn't know what to do because he wasn't ready for marriage. I said, "Look, Mick, if you don't want these problems with girls, then stop sleeping with them!" I quoted the verse above to him and explained that there was something far more than sexual going on when a man and woman perform the act of coitus.

He never altered his behaviour, but even as a non-Christian, he seemed to understand what I was saying. After all, sex is a profoundly personal and intimate interaction between two people. The fact that almost complete strangers would get that vulnerable during a one-night hookup

---

[51] Wilt Chamberlain, *A View from Above* (New York: Penguin Books, 1991), p. 259. In his autobiography Wilt Chamberlain claims to have bedded twenty thousand different women.

should offend our sensibilities when we think about how we generally protect our personal privacy.

If we are really going to comprehend this, we need to go where angels fear to tread. It is no mystery that one of the primary purposes of sex (or consequences, depending on your perspective) is procreation. However, aside from being both procreative and pleasurable, it has a deeper and more significant meaning. All throughout the Bible we read about something called the "blood covenant." When God wanted to enter into an agreement with mankind, something would have to shed blood as a symbol of that covenant. At the Jewish Passover, it was the blood of a lamb (Exodus 12:21). On the Judaic Day of atonement, it was the blood of bulls and goats (Hebrews 9:13). At Jesus' crucifixion, it was His very own blood (Hebrews 9:14).

Cultural anthropologists have discovered that the rite of entering into a blood covenant was common among primitive people.[52] Two tribal chiefs would form an alliance or peace agreement by cutting themselves and drinking the mingled blood. Two warriors might have mingled the blood of their cut wrists to form a blood brotherhood that would bind the two men for life. Even sworn enemies could become blood brothers and then be bound to defend the other person to the point of death. Blood covenants are the single most powerful bond between two people. Unlike a contract or an agreement that may have some form of dissolution clause, the only way out of these blood covenants was death.

At the risk of becoming a bit graphic, every woman is born with a thin, crescent-shaped membrane across the opening of her vagina called the hymen. Science, to this day, has been baffled by the purpose of this strange part of human anatomy. At the occasion of a woman's first sexual encounter, the hymen is broken and a small amount of blood is released. We will often refer to this mysterious event as the moment when a woman loses her virginity. It is not a mystery at all in Scripture. Deuteronomy 22 refers to the blood as the *token* or *evidence* of virginity. If a man married a woman, the blood on the bedsheets was the *evidence of virginity*, proving

---

[52] Melissa L. Meyer, *Thicker than Water: The Origins of Blood as Symbol and Ritual* (New York: Routledge, 2005), p. 3.

that she had never been with another man. The wedding night was a sacred moment where the man and woman entered a blood covenant and became married, for life! This is the explanation for why Jacob had to take his wives' handmaidens as his wives. He had taken their virginity, and as a consequence, entered into a blood covenant with them. Like the sign on the wall in the glassware shop: You break it, you buy it!

Today young people seem to regard virginity as some sort of millstone hanging around their neck that they want to unburden themselves of as quickly as possible. They refer to "losing it" as a badge of honour that they have successfully ridded themselves of some hideous stigma that made them inferior to their peers. It is one of the saddest commentaries on the state of youth culture today because, in reality, they are discarding one of the most precious gifts that God gives to a woman (and her husband). Virginity is the means that God created to initiate a man and a woman into a lifelong blood covenant.

It should make us sad when we see what our sexually-obsessed culture has done with His gift of virginity. And the fact that many Christian young people compromise their virtue and buy into the lie of modern sexual laxity is even sadder. Additionally, our broken, post-Christian Western culture is continually telling young people that if they do not experiment sexually with a variety of different partners, then they are really missing out. Missing out on what?

Nobody ever mentions that the male and female sexual organs are not terribly unique from person to person. There is not much to pick and choose between them. Turns out, one size fits all. In fact, as wonderful as all the human organs are, they are hidden from view on purpose because they are generally so ugly.

Suppose two beautiful kidneys walk into a bar. Which one will get hit on by the handsome liver nursing the martini in the corner booth? It doesn't matter, because there is no such thing as a handsome liver or a beautiful kidney.

Sexuality has almost nothing to do with the actual anatomy and everything to do with what happens when a man and woman connect on the highest level of human intimacy—emotionally, intellectually, hormonally, spiritually and physically. There is nothing outside of marriage that can possibly hold a candle to it.

Biblical Christians have been criticized by some who would say that a perspective like this is completely out of touch with twenty-first century culture and that nobody waits until marriage anymore. This is just not true. I have performed many marriages of young people who have been raised in the church that have respected the gift of virginity and have saved themselves for marriage. More often than not, they will say they are so grateful they waited. They realize that they spared themselves the anguish, grief, guilt or, worse yet, disease or unwanted pregnancy that goes with the territory of sexual promiscuity. They got to share this amazing moment of intimate discovery with the one person alone that they will spend the rest of their life with, without any past baggage inhibiting or haunting them.

Once again, in God's sexual design, there are no shades of grey, only black and white. The only prescribed form of sexuality is within a marriage between a naturally born man and a naturally born woman.[53] We are not going to get into the endless discussion here about the validity of other sexual, marital or relational combinations. There are many Christian and non-Christian writers who are busy debating these issues. If Scripture is your guide, you can read them all and you will still come away unconvinced that God has somehow strayed from His original plan.

Here's how incredibly simply stated it is in Scripture, distilled into three easy points:

1. The original design was one male and one female. *"So God created man in his own image, in the image of God created he him; male and female created he them"* (Genesis 1:27, KJV).[54]

2. God blessed them and told them to have sex and make babies. *"And God blessed them, and God said unto them, Be fruitful,*

---

[53] These are awkward legal descriptions that churches must now use in an age of gender and sexual confusion.

[54] Both were created in the image of God, leading us to conclude that, although God presents Himself in the male gender and in the role of a father, He possesses both male and female characteristics that He divided between the genders.

and multiply, and replenish the earth, and subdue it" (Genesis 1:28, KJV).

3. They obeyed God and it worked. *"And Adam knew Eve his wife; and she conceived, and bare Cain, and said, I have gotten a man from the Lord"* (Genesis 4:1, KJV).

Nowhere in Scripture do we see God deviating from this design. By the time of the Gospels, Jesus was still endorsing the original model using the exact same language.

> *Have you not read that He who made them at the beginning "made them male and female," and said, "For this reason a man shall leave his father and mother and be joined to his wife, and the two shall become one flesh"? So then, they are no longer two but one flesh. Therefore what God has joined together, let not man separate.*
>
> —Matthew 19:4–6

Thousands of years later, Jesus was still going with the one male, one female version of marriage. Anything else is just *fifty shades of black*. Again, we cannot take the examples of Jacob or David or Solomon as biblical endorsements. We have to go with what the Bible actually teaches, not with the mistakes that biblical characters may have made along the way.

Leviticus 18:6–30 carefully delineates the *shades of black* in a very long list of the prohibited sexual practices. Far from saying that they are natural or normal, the Lord calls every last one of them abominations. He does, however, say they are common among the other nations that do not know their Creator. Examples can be readily seen in secular history, as the shocking levels of sexual promiscuity within the Roman and Ancient Greek empires have been well documented.[55] Although these distant cul-

---

[55] "Sexuality in Ancient Rome," Wikipedia (Wikimedia Foundation, May 6, 2020), https://en.wikipedia.org/wiki/Sexuality_in_ancient_Rome. "Homosexuality in Ancient Greece," Wikipedia (Wikimedia Foundation, May 14, 2020), https://en.wikipedia.org/wiki/Homosexuality_in_ancient_Greece.

tures were admittedly far worse than present day North America, it seems we are heading down the very same paths at a dizzying pace.

Before Israel became a nation, God warned the Jewish people that if they engaged in these kinds of sexual practices the land itself would *"vomit them out"* (Leviticus 18:25, NLT). You would have thought that the violent destruction of Sodom and Gomorrah would have already proven as a deterrent (Genesis 13–19), but apparently we are slow learners and in need of constant reminding.

The New Testament gives no evidence of changing the rules.

> *For this is the will of God, your sanctification: that you should abstain from sexual immorality; that each of you should know how to possess his own vessel in sanctification and honor, not in passion of lust, like the Gentiles who do not know God…*
>
> —1 Thessalonians 4:3–5

The Greek word translated "sexual immorality," above, is *porneia*, from which we get our English word pornography. Of all of God's creation, it is hard to think of one thing that has been more corrupted than human sexuality. The entire narrative of Scripture, from beginning to end, is littered with stories of sexual impropriety. Why is that? Because we were created as highly passionate beings, biologically and emotionally inclined to desire sex. Sex was God's idea, and to make sure it happened he gave man an overactive libido and placed him in the world's first nudist colony right next to a naked woman. The Garden of Eden was intended to be a very amorous place.

Someone once told me that Adam was the world's first Mennonite. When I asked him why he would say that, he said, "Who else could stand beside a naked woman and be tempted by an apple?" I think the guy's name was Abe Friesen if you want to write him and complain about that joke.

It was the fall of man that messed this all up. As a result of the sin of Adam and Eve, everything that was created good now has a corrupted alternative as well. The corrupted desire for prosperity is called greed, the desire to overeat is called gluttony, and the unhealthy desire for sex is called lust. Because man has now become a fallen creature with limited spiritual resources, these primal urges have become incredibly hard to tame. Unrestrained, these desires will always lead mankind down a self-destructive path.

It is interesting that the first thing God did with Adam and Eve after the fall was to put clothes on them. It was as if He was saying, "Oh boy, now they've done it! We had better cover them up to give them a fighting chance."

Being a follower of Jehovah/Jesus in a fallen, sexually perverse world will always be a challenge. Even the best and brightest, like Solomon, David, Samson, and others, have not always fared well. And there has never before been a culture with such pervasive temptations as today. We are bombarded by sexuality wherever we turn: television, magazines, fiction, movies and the unregulated tease monster called the internet. No generation has ever had to deal with such easy access to such excessive sexual content. However, this is no excuse, because let us not forget that we also have access to the Holy Spirit working in us and through us, which Jacob, David and Solomon did not have.

One day I was talking with one of my young-adult daughters. She was asking me about something I had referenced in a sermon one day. I told her I knew exactly where to find it online and said, "Just type in [blank-blank-blank].com." It turned out I had given her the wrong web address, and to our complete and utter shock, it went straight to some graphic porn site. She closed it instantly and turned to me and said, "That was easily your worst parenting moment ever." I am not sure I want to take the blame for what happened, as it was an accident, but it definitely was our worst father/daughter moment. And every once in a while, she reminds me of it.

We probably spend way too much time condemning sexual sin and not nearly enough time extolling sexual appropriateness. If we got a better handle on the purpose of sex, we might just figure this whole thing out and stop being such putzes about it.

Far from being merely procreative, sexual passion was designed to bring a husband and wife into a greater depth of intimacy.

One of the most powerful metaphors of Scripture is that the church is the bride and the Jesus is the Bridegroom. In Ephesians 5, the Apostle Paul compares the love a man has for his wife to the love Christ has for us. At first, it sounds like he is merely giving marital advice, telling men they should *"love their wives as their own bodies"* (5:28), etc. but then, out of the blue, he says, *"This is a great mystery, but I speak concerning Christ and the church"* (5:32). In other words, he was saying that marriage is an earthly type, or model, of the relationship between us and Christ. I like to put it this way: marriage is the closest earthly facsimile of the relationship we will have with Christ in heaven. The intimacy we can experience with our spouses on earth is the nearest thing to the ecstasy we will encounter the moment we enter the gates of Heaven. Of course, it will not be sexual at all in nature but ecstatic, nonetheless.

Far from being merely procreative, sexual passion was designed to bring a husband and wife into a greater depth of intimacy. It is critical for married couples to not let sexual intimacy peter out. It is no mystery why it happens, what with the demands of children, the lack of privacy they bring, the busyness of life, domestic tiredness, and the list goes on and on. But one of the biggest factors is the emotional disconnect that affects many marriages. Husbands sometimes don't realize how important the emotional side of the relationship is for their wives. They get their rockets fired up and are ready for blast-off, not recognizing that maybe they should have spent some time preparing the launch pad.

This common scenario is addressed in Paul's first epistle to the Corinthians.

Let the husband render to his wife the affection due her, and likewise also the wife to her husband. The wife does not have authority over her own body, but the husband does. And likewise the husband does not have authority over his own body, but the wife does. Do not deprive one another except with consent for a time, that you may give yourselves to fasting and prayer; and come together again so that Satan does not tempt you because of your lack of self-control.

—1 Corinthians 7:3–5

He says a husband needs to remember to fulfil his wife's need for affection, and vice versa. And, likewise, they each need to consider the other's sexual needs. Notice how the emotional needs of the wife are mentioned first before the husband's, and then Paul reverses the order and mentions the sexual needs of the husband first. I don't believe that was an accident; that's about the way it usually is. Paul further goes on to say when a spouse is deprived sexually, the couple is now at risk of being tempted.

As we age, interest may wane as hormone levels begin to decrease. Couples with a healthy sex life are not at all vulnerable to the temptations of adultery, neither sexually nor emotionally. On the other hand, once the passions of sexual desire flame out they become very difficult to rekindle.

At a men's conference one weekend, the speaker got onto the subject of sexual intimacy. He then posed to the group of men the awkward question publicly, "How many of you lucky dogs are having sex every night?" A few of the younger men raised their hands. Then he asked how many a few times a week. Quite a few hands went up. Then he asked about once a week and got a bunch more. On the question of once a month, a few slightly embarrassed men raised their hands. Finally, he asked if there were any men in the room for whom it was only once a year.

A lone man jumped to his feet, shouting excitedly, "YEAH, THAT'S ME! WOO-HOO!" A bit surprised, the speaker thanked him for his honesty but asked him why he was so excited about it. The man, still teeming with energy, said, "Why am I so excited? BECAUSE TO-NIGHT'S-THE-NIGHT!"

The sheer volume of scriptures that deal with sexual passion would surprise most people. There are literally hundreds of verses and stories on the subject, both good and bad. This is because man was created a sexual being and it would be unthinkable to give us such a strong desire and then not provide instructions as to what to do with it. One of the clearest scriptures has to do with the marriage bed. Hebrews 13:4 says, *"Marriage is honorable among all, and the bed undefiled; but fornicators and adulterers God will judge."* There is nothing sinful in sexual activities for a married couple, providing it does not become dangerous, unhealthy or un-con-senting. Bill and Pam Farrel, who travel and speak on this subject, call it red-hot monogamy.[56]

When it comes to these sexual passions within marriage, King Solomon might actually be helpful for a change, as he wrote an entire book on the act of sex. (Lord knows he had the experience.) The Song of Songs, sometimes called the Song of Solomon, is a poem written entirely in metaphorical language about the wedding night between a man and his virgin wife. Even though the language is a bit cryptic, the book is so sexually charged that, in the Jewish culture, only married men, or at least those of age, were permitted to read it.

There have been several distinct interpretations of the Song of Songs throughout Church history.[57] Many commentators have chosen to interpret it allegorically, to be about Christ's love for the church.[58] This interpretation is nothing new and goes back to the early days of Christianity and to church fathers such as Origen.[59] Still, I am less convinced, because the sexuality is just so pronounced it seems almost a bit creepy to spiritualize it. It is, however, entirely possible, and even probable, that, like many difficult passages in Scripture, it has a double reference to the earthly and to the spiritual. Nevertheless, I want to touch briefly on some of the clearly sexual meanings.

---

[56] Bill Farrel and Pam Farrel, *Red-Hot Monogamy* (Eugene, OR: Harvest House Publishers, 2006).

[57] J. Paul Tanner, "The History of Interpretation of the Song of Songs," Bibliotheca Sacra 154: 613 (1997): 23-46., January 1, 1997, http://biblicalstudies.org.uk/article_song1_tanner. html#17.

[58] Mike Bickle has done a fine job of this with his book *The Song of Songs* (Forerunner Books, 2007).

[59] Origen produced a ten-volume commentary on the book, championing the allegorical interpretation of Song of Songs.

The real hero of the Song of Songs may well be the bride, not the groom, as she actually saved herself for marriage: *"A garden enclosed Is my sister, my spouse, A spring shut up, A fountain sealed"* (4:12). Her garden has never before been entered. A fountain sealed is no doubt the fact that she has kept her virginity intact until this moment. The reference to *my sister* does not mean she was a relative; is merely poetic for the opposite sex. Much of the narrative is from her perspective. She is not named but only identified as a Shulamite woman. This is the only place the term is used in Scripture, so we really cannot say for sure who she was or where she was from.

The story does give us a few clues as to the kind of woman she was, however. She is described as being very beautiful, being dark skinned and possibly even black. *"Do not look upon me, because I am dark, Because the sun has tanned me. My mother's sons were angry with me; They made me the keeper of the vineyards, But my own vineyard I have not kept"* (Song of Songs 1:6). This has persuaded some commentators to conclude that she was, in fact, the Queen of Sheba, but there is nothing else in the narrative that would lead us to believe that. The text indicates she was not likely royalty but a commoner who worked in her brother's vineyards.

It would seem the powerful and rich King Solomon spotted a beautiful ebony young woman working in her family's fields. He took her as yet another of his wives—maybe even a favourite, given the amount of press she receives. The poem seems to record the sexual activity of the wedding night in great detail, using metaphors of fruits and vegetables. I know… it's bizarre, but somehow it works.

Every married couple should read this book together, preferably while in bed, as there is a good chance you won't get through it, if you know what I mean. It's that steamy. I don't want to ruin the surprise for you, but let me give you a brief glimpse.

First, there is a lot of kissing going on. *"Let him kiss me with the kisses of his mouth—For your love is better than wine"* (Song of Solomon 1:2). And it gets pretty hot and heavy: *"Your lips, O my spouse, Drip as the honeycomb; Honey and milk are under your tongue"* (4:11). Then comes the heavy petting: *"My beloved put his hand By the latch of the door, And my heart yearned for him"* (5:4). There are lots of references to the "bits and pieces" (anatomical terminology that I picked up in Junior High School) that are mostly left to our imagination but not a stretch to figure out. Here are a few: *"cakes of raisins"* (2:5); *"orchard of pomegranates"* and *"pleasant fruits"* (4:13); *"grape blossoms"* (7:12); *"twins of a gazelle"* (4:5)—which he specifically identifies as breasts (I would not have guessed that, so I am glad he told us); *"heap of wheat"* (7:2)—which was her belly; *"rounded goblet"* (7:2)—which was her navel... you get the idea. There are a few crypto-erotic (I made that word up) lines that I will leave entirely to your imagination. *"I sat down in his shade with great delight, And his fruit was sweet to my taste"* (2:3), and *"Let my beloved come to his garden And eat its pleasant fruits"* (4:16). I was sweating just typing them all out. There is a lot of talk of what seems like bodily fluids: milk, honey, wine, etc.

At any rate, it sounds like they were having a really good time. An encounter like this was designed to bring two people together into an extraordinary level of intimacy. It is a shame to me that so many people have reduced sexuality to the lurid and lustful image portrayed in pop culture.

There is a very important expression that the Shulamite repeats three times. She says, *"I charge you, O daughters of Jerusalem, Do not stir up nor awaken love Until it pleases"* (Song of Solomon 8:4). Eugene Peterson, in his version, *The Message*, translates it this way: *"Don't excite love, don't stir it up, until the time is ripe—and you're ready."* She is warning the other virgins of Jerusalem to wait until the time is right. Some commentators[60] believe that it was a reference to Solomon trying to bed her before marriage. This is why she is the heroine of the story. She was unwilling to compromise her virtue and was emphatic with others that they, too, should wait for the appropriate time of marriage; if they did, it would be so worth the wait.

The Song of Songs does not hold back in the least regarding the expression of sexual passion, but at the same time it keeps it firmly reserved within the confines of the marriage bed, where God intended it to be. When it comes to the biblical understanding of sex, there are no fifty shades of grey, just black and white.

---

60   Steven G. Cook, The Shulamite and the Shepherd: a Verse-by-Verse Commentary on the Song of Solomon (Bloomington, IN: AuthorHouse, 2004), p. 46. Accessed online at http://www.scook.org/files/shulamite___shepherd.pdf.

Chapter Eleven

Children and Other Hazards of Sex

Insanity is hereditary; you get it from your children.

—Sam Levenson

Someone once said that sex may have been God's way of tricking us into having children. If you had to order them off Amazon, how many would anyone really have? One? Maybe two, if they offered free shipping.

As already stated, the very first command in Scripture is to *"Be fruitful and multiply; fill the earth and subdue it"*(Genesis 1:28). If you think about it, it is the only command we have been able to keep. And we are killing it—seven billion people and counting. If anything, having children is too easy. You do not have to be smart, married or even barely an adult to do it. Five minutes of fun and games, and a brand new person is entering the world and you, the parents, don't have a hot clue what to do when they come. They come without an instruction manual; you do not have to pass any kind of written test; and though they look like they come completely assembled, nothing could be further from the truth. What they are when they first come into this world and what they end up becoming are two entirely different things. You have no way of knowing if they will be a doctor, a lawyer, an Indian chief; a butcher, a baker, a candlestick maker… although you had better pray they are not the last one if you don't want to support them for their entire lives.

Parenting will most likely be the most difficult thing that we do with our lives. When we bring home a newborn, they are completely and utterly dependent upon us twenty-four hours a day. They are ridiculous. They can't eat for themselves, change themselves or think for themselves;

they can't even hold their own head up. You think, "God, what have you done to me? How am I going to even keep this thing alive?" Yet, somehow, we figure it out and, most of the time, manage not to kill them.

The journey is full of ironies. You spend the first three years of their lives trying to get them to walk and talk, and then the next three, trying to get them to sit down and shut up. In terms of investment, there is nothing in this world that you will devote more time, energy and heartache to then your children.

Consequently, if there is one thing we need to be passionate about in life it should be our children. In the Old Testament the first thing God said to us was to *"be fruitful and multiply,"* while the last thing He said was,

Behold, I will send you Elijah the prophet
Before the coming of the great and dreadful day of the Lord.
And he will turn
The hearts of the fathers to the children,
And the hearts of the children to their fathers,
Lest I come and strike the earth with a curse.

—Malachi 4:5–6

The last thing people say is often the most important. Before the four hundred years of prophetic silence between the Old Testament and New Testament, God said He was going to restore the passion of the fathers for their children. He also said that the consequence of us not responding was that He would smite the earth with a curse.

There is nothing in the world that compares to the family as a foundation that holds a society together. As goes the family, so goes the nation.

When my generation was being born, in the fifties and sixties, fathers were barely involved in the process. Our dads impregnated our mothers and then, with a manly grunt, proclaimed, "My work here is done." Nine months later, they dropped our mothers off at the hospital on the way to work. They returned at 5 p.m. with a box of cigars to see how it was going. They never entered the birthing room but lingered outside in a waiting room with other fathers and talked about fishing and wondered why it was taking so long. Meanwhile, in the obstetrics ward, Mom lay in the bed half-conscious, doped up on powerful narcotics, waiting for the obstetrician to get back from his golf game. When he finally arrived, he knocked her right out with some even stronger drugs and pulled the baby out with a pair of forceps. This left a big dent in either side of your skull that finally disappeared sometime when you were in the fifth grade. The doctor then emerged to tell the father he had a boy (or girl) and that Mommy was doing just fine but might have to sleep off the drugs for the next few weeks… or years. Then Dad went out for drinks and cigars with the new friends he met in the waiting room.

This has all changed today. There will be no drinks and cigars. Today's modern father is as involved as the mother and is required by law to go to a minimum of three hundred prenatal classes. Here, the expectant father will watch terrifying videos of babies being born, in order to desensitize them of the horror of seeing blood and guts spewing out of their wife's nether region. Together they will learn the fine art of baby-delivery-breathing. This is important because his wife will not be given any of the really great drugs of the past and will be overcoming the pain only by the careful systematic rhythm of breathing. But, given her level of discomfort, she will not remember how to do the breathing or even whether to breathe at all, so it will be up to young husband to coach her through this. He, of course, will be of no use because he wasn't really paying attention during the classes, as he was playing on his brand new iPhone which has some amazing new features. "Have you seen the new iPhone?" There is a lot of blood, sweat, tears, wailing and gnashing of teeth… and I understand it is uncomfortable for the woman as well. In the end, a baby the size of a watermelon magically appears out of an opening closer to the size of a golf ball. The father now needs to go on paternity leave for six months or a year to recover from the ordeal… oh, and to help parent the newborn. All sarcasm aside, it is truly an encouraging turn of events that the modern father is taking such an interest in his children. It means there is still hope for the family.

There is nothing in the world that compares to the family as a foundation that holds a society together. As goes the family, so goes the nation. However, the construct of the family has gone through many incarnations. To argue that the *nuclear family* (husband, wife and a couple of children) is the historic norm, and that it has always been so, would be somewhat inaccurate. The *extended family* (husband, wife, children, Grandma, Grandpa, brother and his wife and kids, dopey single uncle, and in some cases, servants or slaves) would have been more common in history and still is in Southern European, Arab, Asian, Latin and many African cultures.

The nuclear family is more of an Anglo-Saxon creation that dates back to the thirteenth century.[61] Unlike in Southern Europe, where a young man would remain in or marry into the "family home," in England they would marry later in life after they had saved enough money to set up an independent home. In those days, life expectancies were also shorter and multi-generational households were a rarity, as grandparents did not live into old age. Because couples were marrying later in life, they often had fewer children than did their southern European counterparts that began procreating sooner. However, the nuclear family proved to be very successful because it was agile and able to adapt to the ever-changing economic eventualities of the world. During the Industrial Revolution, for example, families did not need eight children to run the farm, as dad worked instead in the factory and was able to support his leaner version of family.

The family is a dynamic institution that has had to evolve with the social and economic realities of the times. The twentieth century saw the family take it on the chin. It began with World War I, which created millions of widows and orphans. And then, before the family had time to recover, they found themselves in the midst of the Great Depression. The unemployment and lower wages of the 1930s forced North Americans to delay marriage and having children. Divorce was almost non-existent

---

[61] Kay Hymowitz, "The Real Roots of the Nuclear Family," Institute for Family Studies, December 23, 2013, https://ifstudies.org/blog/the-real-roots-of-the-nuclear-family.

because nobody could afford that luxury. The woman and children had no option but to find part time work just to enable the family to feed itself. No sooner did the Depression end, than millions of fathers and sons were once again sent overseas to fight in World War II. Many did not return. The women ran the households alone and went into the factories to support the war industries. The "latchkey kid" was born, and juvenile delinquency, unwed pregnancy and truancy all rose dramatically.[62]

The post-war era saw some sense of normality return to the North American family. As the economy recovered, young couples began to marry earlier again (women at around twenty years old), the birth rate doubled and the nuclear family of father, mother and a few kids returned as the cultural norm. It was idealized as the model family in the mid-twentieth century by TV shows like *Leave it to Beaver*. Ward and June Cleaver had two sons: Wally and Theodore (The Beaver). Ward went off to work, while mom stayed home and kept the house and managed the boys. The Beav was portrayed as a naïve Tom-Sawyer-like character who always kept life interesting. Families sat down together after supper and watched the weekly episodes on black and white televisions. It was a quieter and simpler time for the family.

Now, in the twenty-first century, the majority of families no longer look anything like the Cleavers. We have blended families, single parent families, working families (where both parents have careers), and a host of other new and interesting combinations. Irrespective of the configuration, the family as an institution is once again under siege. In Western cultures we are seeing a social experiment in play, where the state is assuming the responsibility for raising the next generation.

A few years ago, my wife, Kathy, travelled to Paris with her sister on a vacation. They visited all the famous and beautiful sites like the Eifel Tower and the Arc de Triomphe. As they toured this extraordinary city, something caught her notice. There were no children anywhere in sight.

---

[62]   cpsonline, "The Evolution of American Family Structure," Concordia University, St. Paul Online, June 23, 2015, https://online.csp.edu/blog/family-science/the-evolution-of-american-family-structure.

Kathy is a mother at heart and will always notice the children wherever we go, whereas I am not likely to notice one way or another.

Upon further investigation she discovered where the children were. Although public school is mandatory by age six, most Parisians send their kids off to school by age two or three. Not only that, many of the schools will keep the children until dinner hours so that the parents can dine out after work. New education legislation also mandates that the schools may not assign any homework, so as not to burden the parents, who will only have an hour or two with their children each night before bed anyway.[63] It is not clear what the long-term outcome will be for the French experiment, but if we can believe what the prophet Malachi has to say, it won't be great.

From unhelpful political interference, to unfavourable tax legislation, to the unending attempts to redefine the family and the unrelenting pressure from radical feminism, the historic understanding of the family seems to be under continual attack. The good news is that the family will survive. It always does. It is the bedrock of any stable culture. It is more important than good government, good economy, or even good Wi-Fi. Even with all the prevailing forces mounting up against the traditional family, God seems to be turning the hearts of fathers towards their children, just as He said He would do in the book of Malachi.

---

[63]   Adam Sage, "French Children Are Promised an End to Homework," *The Times*, June 9, 2017, https://www.thetimes.co.uk/article/french-children-are-promised-an-end-to-homework-25wbcjwzp.

Chapter Twelve

The Passionate Parent

It is easier to build strong children than to repair broken men.
—Frederick Douglass

When it comes to children, there are no hard and fast guarantees that your kids will turn out well. You can do everything right (although you won't) and still have kids that go astray. However, there are things that you can do that will greatly increase your chances of having great kids.

Like everything else in life, success in child-rearing is multi-factorial; there is no one single magic bullet. It is not, however, so elusive and onerous that nobody can achieve it. In fact, parents who are really passionate about their families will do many things right instinctively.

The acrostic I use to describe passionate parenting is K.I.D.S.

Keeping Kids a Value
Instilling Your Virtues
Developing a Family Vision
Staying Vigilant

1. Keeping Kids a Value

In the 1970s, J. Paul Getty was the world's richest man. In 1973, his sixteen-year-old grandson J. Paul Getty III was kidnapped in Rome by an organized crime ring. I remember it well because I was exactly the same age as the younger Paul and the story was being covered on the nightly news. In 2017, Ridley Scott recreated the drama in the movie *All the Money in the World.* He took a few liberties with the story, like Hollywood does, but he got it reasonably close. I thought it was a worthwhile subject to revisit all these years later because it shines a bright light on family values… or the lack thereof.

When the kidnappers demand a ransom of $17 million, Getty's estranged daughter-in-law asks him if he would pay the ransom. He steadfastly refuses claiming that he does not have the means to do so and that paying off kidnappers only encourages it as a criminal activity. The most startling line in the movie happens when a reporter asks Getty a loaded question: if he would not pay $17 million for the release of his grandson, how much would he pay? Getty says, "Nothing!" and then turns and walks away.

As the drama drags out, grandson Paul is kept hostage in a remote location in Italy and weeks go by without any ransom being paid. The kidnappers grow impatient and sell their captive to another crime organization. They lower the ransom to four million dollars, but Getty still won't pay it. He finally agrees to contribute one million dollars, because that is the maximum amount he can claim as tax deductible. Only after the kidnappers cut off young Paul's ear and mail it to a newspaper, does Getty agree to pay the full ransom. That is the movie version of the events.

In real life, according to John Pearson's book, on which the film is based, Getty Sr. paid $2.2 million towards the ransom, as his accountants told him that was the amount that would be tax-deductible as a casualty loss under the tax code of the day. The boy's father, J. Paul Getty II, came up with the other $1.8 million, which he did by borrowing from his father Getty Sr. at four percent interest.[64] No joke! The truth is almost stranger than the fiction. In the end, the boy made it home safely, minus one ear, but it is a bizarre story. What kind of family decides what a child's life is worth based on a tax deduction?

---

64   Olivia B. Waxman, "All the Money in the World True Story: The Getty Kidnapping" (*Time*, December 25, 2017), http://time.com/5068192/getty-kidnapping-history.

In biblical times, a man's family was his greatest treasure and of the highest value. This is the predominate understanding of true wealth throughout all the Scriptures.

Contrast this story with that of Jesus' parable of the Prodigal Son. It is considered by many to be the *Prince of Parables* and arguably the most important theological illustration that Jesus gave.

The story begins with a successful father and his two sons. The youngest demands his inheritance early and leaves the family ranch to go discover himself. He spends the entire wad on wine, women and song and then finds himself completely destitute. He takes a job on a lowly and culturally shameful pig farm. There he was, waist deep in the pig slop and longing to eat the pods the swine were eating, when he came to his senses and had a thought: after how he had wasted the family fortune, there would be no way his dad would welcome him back into the fold, but maybe, just maybe, he would let him become a servant. After all, his father's servants lived better than he was doing.

The wayward son decides to return home and beg his father for a job in the stables. As we read the narrative, we witness one of the most powerful moments in Scripture: *"But when he was still a great way off, his father saw him and had compassion, and ran and fell on his neck and kissed him"* (Luke 15:20).

If his father saw him while he was still a great way off, that could only mean that he was looking for him to return. We can only imagine that every morning the father arose early and peered into the distance to see if there was anyone coming, and on that day, there he was. The father did not sit back and play it cool—maybe give him the cold shoulder for a few days and make him suffer—NO, he RAN to greet him and threw himself upon his wayward son, kissing his swine-slop-stinking neck. Immediately, he calls for the best robe, a ring for his finger and sandals for his feet. (All three of these things were symbols of belonging to the family. Servants would not have any of these things, only a favoured son.) The father then called a feast and ordered the killing of the fatted calf.

Well, for some reason the killing of the fatted calf is a bone of contention for the older brother, who would not attend the feast. When the father asks him what the problem is, the brother claims that he never even got a young goat to make merry with his friends, let alone the coveted fatted calf. Dad tries to calm him down, reminding him that all he owns has always been at his disposal, and explaining, *"your brother was dead and is alive again, and was lost and is found"* (Luke 15:32).

Properly interpreted, this parable was told for the sake of the Pharisees, who did not understand why Jesus was a "friend of sinners." It is theologically important, as it epitomizes the extraordinary message of the grace of God; none of us have strayed so far that we would not be welcomed back into the family of God. The intention is that we should see ourselves, not as the father, but as the prodigal son. Those among us of a rigid religious nature are to see themselves as the angry older son who does not understand the grace of God. It is the Prince of Parables for good reason, but it is still a story of a father who understood what his true values were. He never even asked what the son did with the money. He never asked if he had any of it left—He didn't care. The money was of no value to him whatsoever; all he wanted was his son back. And he would have gladly paid *all the money in the world*.

In biblical times, a man's family was his greatest treasure and of the highest value. This is the predominate understanding of true wealth throughout all the Scriptures. King Solomon put it this way: *"Children's children are the crown of old men, And the glory of children is their father"* (Proverbs 17:6). In the midst of all his wealth and accomplishment he still seemed to understand that his children and grandchildren were his greatest crowning achievement. We do not know how many children Solomon had (it is entirely possible he didn't know either), but with the one thousand wives and concubines we can assume that it was in the multiple thousands.

There is somewhat of a modern-day Solomon living in the Mizoram state of India. Ziona Chana is claimed to be the father of the world's largest family. He is married to thirty-nine wives and has ninety-four children, fourteen daughters-in-law and thirty-three grandchildren for a total of 180… and counting. As the founder of his own "Christian" sect, he can make his own rules as to how many wives he is allowed. They live in a huge one-hundred-room hotel-like four-story home where his wives sleep in giant communal dormitories. This is how he describes his good fortune, "Today I feel like God's special child. He's given me so many people to look after. I consider myself a lucky man to be the husband of 39 women and head of the world's largest family."[65] Few of us could even imagine being that "wealthy."

I remember one day I was preaching on the family and made this wisecrack, "What is the difference between a man with ten million dollars and a man with ten children? Answer; the man with ten children doesn't want any more!"

After the service an upset woman came up to me and asked, "So, which one of my eleven children should I not have had?"

Still on a roll, I replied, "I don't know… I have not met all your children." She did not find that funny either.

Few of us will have our family values tested to the level of J. Paul Getty or the prodigal's father, but at some level we are tested every day. We make judgment calls with our time and our money continually without giving it much thought.

My own father was a very generous man who would likely give you the shirt off his back if you needed it. Yet, on another level, he often missed out on the finer details of parenthood. He routinely went off to the office on Sunday afternoon instead of spending "unproductive" time with his six kids. When we asked him why he had to work on Sunday he would say, "I need to keep the wolf away from the door." In his mind putting food on the table was the most important way for him to show his love for his family. That was not uncommon for men of his generation, who lived through the Great Depression. His motive was pure, but in

---

65   Daily Mail Reporter, "The World's Biggest Family: Ziona Chan Has 39 Wives, 94 Children and 33 Grandchildren," *Daily Mail Online* (Associated Newspapers, February 8, 2016), http://www.dailymail.co.uk/news/article-1358654/The-worlds-biggest-family-Ziona-Chan-39-wives-94-children-33-grandchildren.html#ixzz55IgOjsbQ.

retrospect, he worked way too much—he didn't need to, he chose to. It was his preeminent value. We were not going to starve to death; he was a lawyer, for goodness sake.

2. Instilling Your Virtues

Maybe it was because he was always at work, but my father never had the sex talk with me. He left that responsibility to my mother, whose approach was less than adequate. She gave me a book called *The Birds and the Bees*. It was literally about birds and bees and did not mention human sexuality at all. After I read the twenty-page book, complete with pictures of *birds* and *bees,* she asked me if I understood it.

I replied. *"Yeah!"* Then she asked if I had any questions and I said, "No."

She said, "Good talk, son." and that was it. I was no more aware of the concept of human procreation than I was before the book and the following talk.

Thank God for my thirteen-year-old friend Blair. He was a self-proclaimed expert on sex. He was widely experienced and highly knowledgeable on the subject. He sat down with me after school one day and explained the whole thing in graphic detail. My eyes were like saucers as he described the intricacies of the female anatomy. After about two hours he asked if I understood it.

I replied, *"Yeah!"* Then he asked if I had any questions and I said, "No."

He said, "Good talk, Mark."

There was only one small problem with Blair's lesson on sex. He was almost one hundred percent inaccurate on every detail. Turned out, he did not know what he was talking about. Boy, was I surprised on our wedding night! Nevertheless, by some chance we still managed to fulfil the first of God's commands and have three children. It all comes quite naturally, actually; you can do it without a book or a Blair.

But imagine my shock when our youngest daughter threw out the big question at only age seven. She said, "Hey, I have question. Where do babies come from anyway?"

I was so completely thrown off guard that I hummed and hawed and stumbled, and then finally I said, "Why don't you ask your mother?"

She looked up at me and said in disbelief, "You don't know either, do you?"

To which I quickly responded, "No, I don't. Ask your mother; she might know."

Here is King Solomon's advice for mothers and fathers on the subject of instilling values:

Hear, my children, the instruction of a father,
And give attention to know understanding...

—Proverbs 4:1

A child left to himself brings shame to his mother.

—Proverbs 29:15

In simpler terms, he said that the father has a responsibility to instruct his children in righteousness, and if he doesn't, the mother will likely take the blame. Sounds about right!

One of the most interesting historical comparisons made between two families has been that of Jonathan Edwards and Max Juke. An online search will find dozens of versions of the story with wildly varying details, so one needs to be careful not to misrepresent the facts. However, the contrast between one determinedly godly family and one generally criminal one is staggering. Jonathan Edwards was born in Connecticut in 1703. He attended Yale University at the age of fourteen and later became a leading author, philosopher, theologian and revivalist preacher. He is best known for his sermon "Sinners in the hands of an angry God." He was a key player in the Great Awakening and saw thousands of people come to Christ in the early 1700s. He founded a college that today is Princeton University. His life was extraordinarily accomplished.

His historical contemporary, Max Juke, was a world class deadbeat. He became the subject of a study by sociologist Richard L. Dugdale in 1877 called, *The Jukes: A Study in Crime, Pauperism, Disease and Heredity.* It all began in 1874, when Dugdale was asked to inspect thirteen county jails in upstate New York. He was surprised to discover that many of the inmates were related by blood or marriage to one family. For the sake of anonymity, he gave this family a pseudonym of "the Jukes" and named the patriarch, who was born in 1720, Max Juke. His real name has been more recently been revealed as Max Keyser.[66]

Over the years various people have compared the family legacies of Johnathan Edwards and Max Juke/Keyser. The most accurate is probably the 1900 publication by A. E. Winship.[67] This is how it breaks down:

Jonathan Edwards

1394 total descendants

100 lawyers

100 clergymen

80 politicians

75 military officers

60 physicians

60 authors

30 judges

13 college presidents

3 city mayors

3 state governors

3 senators

1 vice president of USA

[66]   Scott Christianson, "Bad Seed or Bad Science?" (*The New York Times*, February 8, 2003), tp://www.nytimes.com/2003/02/08/arts/bad-seed-or-bad-science.html.

    E. Winship, *Jukes-Edwards A Study in Education and Heredity* (Urbana, Illinois: Project nberg, 2005), retrieved June 4, 2020, from www.gutenberg.org/ebooks/15623.

Max Juke

1200 total descendants (approx.)

300 died in infancy.

310 paupers

130 criminals

60 habitual thieves

50 prostitutes

7 murderers

The original motive for making this comparison was not a noble one, with some writers trying to make an argument for eugenics, claiming that certain families were genetically morally inferior or superior. This is, of course, ridiculous. The Juke family was obviously handicapped by poverty, the lack of education and opportunity.

However, the comparison between these two legacies is not unfair when taken from the perspective of parenting. Historically and biblically, good parenting produces good results and negligent parenting engenders bad results. The Bible explicitly says, *"For I, the Lord your God, am a jealous God, visiting the iniquity of the fathers upon the children to the third and fourth generations of those who hate Me"* (Exodus 20:5). The Juke family is certainly proof of this principle.

In the March 1902 issue of *The School Journal*, the writer made this extreme claim: "The almost universal traits of the 'Jukes' were idleness, ignorance and vulgarity. These characteristics led to disease and disgrace, to pauperism and crime."[68] In comparison, the Edwards clan has gone down in history as among the most eminent of all-American families.

Instilling our virtues into our kids is one of the biggest responsibilities we will ever take on in life. It will not happen by osmosis—it will

---

[68]   Robert L. Meyers, "Does the Community get the Worth of the Money it Expends on the Schools," *The School Journal*, Volume 64 (E.L. Kellogg & Company, March 8, 1902), p. 280. Retrieved from Google Books on June 4, 2020, at https://books.google.com/books?id=kadLAAAAYAAJ&printsec=frontcover&dq=The+School+Journal,+Volume+64+page+280&hl=en&sa=X&ved=0ahUKEwig-rKN4__YAhXNzVMKHanDDU-UQ6AEILTAB#v=onepage&q&f=false.

require an ongoing relational connection with our kids at every age of their development. Most parents do a reasonably good job during the younger ages but start to lose contact with their kids as they get older. Many parents lose a meaningful connection by the time their kids are teens; they have unwittingly allowed their children to be influenced more by their friends then by their parents, not unlike what happened to me with my idiot friend Blair.

Gordon Neufeld and Gabor Mate have written a very insightful book on the subject, entitled, *Hold on to your Kids; Why Parents Need to Matter More Than Peers.*[69] Their thesis is that kids today can be most influenced by a "peer orientation" or a "family orientation." They warn today's parents that many are allowing their kids' peers to be the primary influences in their lives. Parents desperately want their kids to be liked and to have friends, but they often abdicate the role as primary influencer to a group of kids that don't know any better than their own kid. Almost all parents have good intentions for their children, but the authors rightly observe, "Children do not experience our intentions, no matter how heartfelt. They experience what we manifest in tone and behavior."[70]

If we do not deliberately inculcate our virtues into our children, they will by default take on those of their peers. These "young sages" have no ability to produce in one another any of the three big objectives of personal development: a sense of security, individuality or maturity. How can a group of immature adolescents possibly produce maturity in one another? And what could be more insecure than the teenage posse? Cliques form overnight and a teen can find himself (or herself) on the outside just as quickly. As for individuality, it doesn't even exist amongst young people today. They all dress alike, think alike, act alike, etc.

At the risk of going where angels fear to tread, let's talk about tattoos, for example. The number of young people with tattoos will soon be in the

---

[69]   Gordon Neufeld and Maté Gabor, *Hold on to Your Kids: Why Parents Need to Matter More than Peers* (New York: Ballantine Books, 2014).

[70]   Ibid, p. 15.

majority.[71] Yet, when I ask young adults about why they got one, they almost always give me the same answer, "I am expressing my individuality." Or in the case of a pierced tongue, "Imm exprethin mah induhviduality." Tattoos have become the tribal mark of our modern culture. Although I am not a fan of the fad, I am more concerned with the fact that they think that defaulting to the uniformity of their culture is somehow an expression of individuality. If one does something that everyone else is doing, that is, by definition, NOT individuality. Please don't miss the point. A tattoo in and of itself is neither here nor there, but it is emblematic of the primary source of influence for an emerging generation.

I used reverse psychology with my kids on this issue. When my son was four years old, he saw his first tattoo and asked what it was. I explained that it was artwork on the skin that was made by jabbing needles under the skin's surface and injecting ink. I told him it could never be removed because the ink was permanently under the skin. Then I told him that when he turned sixteen I was going to take him to the tattoo parlor and get a tattoo of an anchor on his arm like Popeye the Sailor. He didn't know who Popeye was and he was quite sure he didn't want a tattoo either. Every birthday I reminded him of how many years there were remaining until he got his tattoo, and every year he would say, "I am never getting a tattoo!"

When he finally turned sixteen, I said, "Well, today is the day."

By then he had developed a strong sense of confidence and individuality and calmly stated, "I'm not getting a tattoo!"

I casually responded, "Ok, suit yourself—it's your life."

I am not saying this strategy will work for every parent, but it worked for me.

Parents need to pick their battles carefully. We shouldn't even try to win them all. We need to win the ones that really matter. A short list of these virtues might include: honesty, morality, diligence, discipline and, of course, faith. If we can instill a personal sense of the Christian faith in

---

71   Meredith Newman, "Report: More Young People Have Tattoos and Piercings than Ever Before," *USA Today* (Gannett Satellite Information Network, September 20, 2017), https://www.usatoday.com/story/news/nation-now/2017/09/20/young-people-tattoos-and-piercings-report/686360001.

our kids, most everything else that is really important will follow. It is the reason why many Christian parents today choose to home school or send their children to a Christian school. That may not be an option for every family, but if it is, it is certainly a price worth paying.

The church is the one place still left in our society that will reinforce the virtues we are trying to teach at home.

Perhaps the most important thing we can do is raise our kids in an environment where they have a love for church. The church is the one place still left in our society that will reinforce the virtues we are trying to teach at home. You can always spot the adults that were raised in a church setting as kids. They are often more compassionate, more caring and more conscientious. They will tend to have a greater sense of responsibility and honesty and will be less likely to resort to the vulgarity of speech that has become so ubiquitous in the world today.

Sometimes parenting can feel like an impossible task. You may feel like you are constantly fighting against a Star Trek high-intensity tractor beam that is pulling your kids into its vortex. And just when you think you have a figured a few things out, they have another birthday and everything changes again! But God would not entrust us with a responsibility and not equip us to succeed. These first two principles alone of Keeping Kids a Value and Instilling our Virtues can counteract anything our fallen world throws at us. God is always on our side!

Chapter Thirteen

Cat's in the Cradle and the Silver Spoon

And as I hung up the phone, it occurred to me. He'd grown up just like me. My boy was just like me.

— Harry Chapin, "Cat's in the Cradle"

"Cat's in the Cradle," was Harry Chapin's only number one song. It was a melodic but sad ballad about a father who does not have time for his son while he is growing up. In the second-last verse, the son is all grown up and he has no time for his father. Hence, the line, "He'd grown up just like me, My boy was just like me."

It is pretty much any parent's worst nightmare to think that our children could grow up with all of our worst qualities and none of our best. My mother, whose life-long nickname is Chickie, is famous for making this crack about any one of her six children: "Too bad you got your dad's looks and my brains." It was a humorous insult… at everybody's expense. Passing on our weaknesses is, of course, entirely avoidable, but it will take some concerted effort.

The most famous parenting advice in all of Scripture comes once again from our illustrious King Solomon.

Train up a child in the way he should go,
And when he is old he will not depart from it.

—Proverbs 22:6

Literally translated, "train up a child" means to "initiate a child at the mouth of his path." More simply put, it is to show them the way at the beginning of his journey so that they may possibly continue in that same direction. A perfect example of this, one that likely every North American parent has experienced, is teaching a child to ride a bike. We put them on the bike, point them in the right direction, and then run alongside them. Only when they appear stable do we let go and allow them to continue on their own. This will give them the best chance for early success instead of letting them struggle away on their own, repeatedly falling and crashing into things.

At the beginning we choose the path—usually one free from obstacles like parked cars. As they become more comfortable and competent, they will eventually choose their own path. We hope and pray that our initial example was a good one but, as I said, there are no hard and fast guarantees in parenting. And every parent brings their unique idiosyncrasies into the equation, which make it even more interesting.

When my kids were younger, I wanted to build them a go-kart just like the one my childhood friend Roy and I eventually cut in half (Chapter One). It looked almost identical to the Blue Bomb, only I painted this one black and called it the Black Bart. I even used the same rack and pinion steering that was so temperamental. One Sunday afternoon my friend Keith (a pastor on our staff) came over with his family. We were messing around on the street with the go-kart and I said, "You should take Ben for a ride." Without hesitation, his ten-year-old son Ben climbed into the driver's seat and Keith placed the hockey stick in the slot at the rear to push. Before they departed, I warned Keith that he should go slowly at first to give Ben a chance to get used to the steering. It seemed like he acknowledged the advice and then took off in a mad sprint. Ben had not gone fifty feet before he lost control of the kart and crashed into the curb, launching him through the air and depositing him face-first on the concrete. Ben was bleeding and all scraped up.

I ran over in a sense of urgency to find Keith picking him up without concern. He took one look and said, "He's fine... it'll just toughen him up."

I realized, in that moment, how differently we all parent. Some are more cautious, some stricter, some more lax. (Keith was still a very good parent and has four really great grown kids today.) There is more than one way to skin a *cat… in the cradle*. And the most successful children are not necessarily those who are born with a *silver spoon* in their mouths.

This brings us to the D in our K.I.D.S. acrostic of guiding principles that can help ensure parental success.

3. Developing a Family Vision

Sometimes we hear parents say, "Well, we got the kids through college. Our job is done." If only it were that simple. For many successful families, the journey is now just beginning.

One thing people of the Jewish culture have done well is to develop a family vision for their children that endures, sometimes from generation to generation. How is it that a race that only makes up two percent of the North American population accounts for thirty percent of all jurists on the US Supreme Court, thirty-three percent of the students at Ivy League Universities like Yale and Harvard, thirty-three percent of the professors of those same universities, forty percent of all Nobel Prizes for sciences[72] and ninety-nine percent of the comedians? (Actually, I made that last one up.) Is it because they are statistically smarter than everyone else on the planet? There is no evidence to that effect. What is even more remarkable is that there have been more attempts to eradicate the Jews from the face of the earth than any other race. Maybe it is in part due to that ongoing persecution that they continue to excel and achieve as a people of influence in whatever location they land on the planet, something of a survival instinct.

When parents put certain expectations on their children, it is shocking how often they come to be. There is a joke about a mother bragging to her friends during a Pilates class. "My daughter has been married three times—first a doctor, then a lawyer, now a dentist… so much joy from one child."

Jewish families seem to be acutely in tune to the idea of developing a family vision and passing it on to the next generation. The evidence speaks for itself. Nine times in the Old Testament, we see the Jewish people

---

[72] Jan Van Der Vurst, *Impact - Respect Based Influence* (Leuven, Belgium: Lannoo Publishers, 2012), p. 55.

commanded to pass their faith, culture and material inheritance down to the next generations. Isaiah put it this way, *"Enlarge the place of your tent, And let them stretch out the curtains of your dwellings"* (Isaiah 54:2), and in Proverbs 13:22, King Solomon opined, *"A good man leaves an inheritance to his children's children, But the wealth of the sinner is stored up for the righteous."* A wrong interpretation would be to see this as instruction to leave a monetary fortune to your children so that they can live as trust fund brats. It is much broader than that. It has to include our spiritual heritage, as that is what allows our real influence to endure from generation to generation.

It goes all the way back to Jacob, the very first Jew and father of the nation of Israel. Each of his sons, in turn, was the patriarch of one of the twelve tribes that would inherit the Promised Land. He prophesied over each of his twelve sons what kind of men they would be and the kind of influence they would have in their nation (Genesis 49). Issachar would be farmers, Benjamin would be warriors, Dan would be judges, Levi would be priests, Judah would be rulers and eventually the kings. King David, King Solomon and, of course, Jesus, were all of the line of Judah. Over two thousand years after the blessing of Judah, Jesus came into the world as the King of Kings.

There are some modern-day examples of Jewish legacies that have survived hundreds of years and even outlived the Jewish Holocaust. For example, in the late 1500s the Gradis family, Jewish refugees from Portugal, settled in Bordeaux France. In 1685, they founded the Gradis Corporation wine trading business. The company survived the Seven Years' War of 1756 to 1763 and both World Wars. During WWI, the French government commissioned the family to ensure the supply of sugar for France, which they did, but then they returned to their roots in the wine trading business after the war ended. If you are born a Gradis, there is a pretty good chance you are going to be in the wine trading business. It is a legacy that has lasted an astounding five hundred years.

The point is not that we want our children to necessarily follow in our exact footsteps but that, as parents, we are often in a better place to sense what our children may excel at than they are. We should at least point them in the right direction. And if they decide to "ride their bike in a different direction," at least they had all the best opportunities to make that decision. Families that sacrifice to help their kids go to good schools, colleges and universities have made a very worthwhile investment. It is very difficult in our competitive world for young people to get ahead without a proper education.

We have a Chinese friend who is an eye doctor and a surgeon. Dr. Lee is a delightful person with a South American wife and two wonderful kids. Lee's story is fascinating. He was the son of Chinese immigrants. His parents ran an inner-city grocery story and raised thirteen children. He was number eleven. Lee says that, growing up, their parents drilled into the children the belief that they could be whatever they wanted to be in a nation like Canada. All it would take was good values and hard work. Apparently, the kids believed them because they all grew up to become doctors and engineers and PHDs and various professionals. His parents were not wealthy people and were not able to pay for the kids' post-secondary schooling. They all needed to work at part-time jobs and win scholarships in order to pay their own way through university.

It is an inspiring story but, what impressed me most, was Lee's underlying motivation for why he devoted thirteen years of his life developing a double medical specialty. I interviewed him for this book and asked him what his passion was in life. He said, "My motivation has always been to help other people. I have never cared about the money. I just want to do my part to make the world a better place and give something back for all the blessing my family has received in Canada."

Before you think, "That's what they all say!" consider this: he is the only doctor I know that will do surgery all day long, starting in the early morning, and then, after supper, phone every patient he operated on that day and ask them how they are doing. I know some of his patients personally and they told me that they were shocked when they got the call from their surgeon asking how they were doing. Lee's parents, irrespective of their race, seemed to know a thing or two about parenting and developing a family vision.

Yale University Law professor Amy Chua has written some provocative books on the subject of parenting. She asks the politically incorrect question as to why kids from certain races consistently outperform kids from other races. Chua points out that Indo-Americans earn almost double the national average in wages; Mormons have a disproportionately high number of leaders in corporate America; and that prestigious Stuyvesant High School in New York, which offers admission based solely on a standardized entrance exam, had an enrollment of 177 white students, twenty-four Hispanics, nine blacks and… 620 Asians![73] She claims that many of the Asians are of Chinese origin and are children of restaurant workers and other working-class immigrants. She believes that it has nothing to do with race and everything to do with parenting. She even used her own family as a case in point in her best-selling book *Battle Hymn of the Tiger Mother*. She pokes fun at herself along the way, but is still quite serious.

> This was supposed to be a story of how Chinese parents are better at raising kids than Western ones. But instead, it's about a bitter clash of cultures, a fleeting taste of glory, and how I was humbled by a thirteen-year-old.[74]

Her main point is that Chinese mothers are excessive, obsessive and demanding. She sums it up this way, and she is not really joking.

> A lot of people wonder how Chinese parents raise such stereotypically successful kids. They wonder what these parents do to produce so many math whizzes and music prodigies, what it's like inside the family, and whether they could do it too. Well, I can tell them, because I've done it. Here are some things my daughters, Sophia and Louisa, were never allowed to do:
> - attend a sleepover
> - have a playdate
> - be in a school play

---

[73]   Amy Chua and Jed Rubenfeld, "What Drives Success?" (*The New York Times*, January 25, 2014), https://www.nytimes.com/2014/01/26/opinion/sunday/what-drives-success.html.

[74]   Amy Chua, "Excerpt: 'Battle Hymn of the Tiger Mother'" (*The New York Times*, January 11, 2011), http://www.nytimes.com/2011/01/19/books/excerpt-battle-hymn-of-the-tiger-mother.html.

- complain about not being in a school play
- watch TV or play computer games
- choose their own extracurricular activities
- get any grade less than an A
- not be the #1 student in every subject except gym and drama
- play any instrument other than the piano or violin
- not play the piano or violin.[75]

As I was writing this, and thinking how ridiculous it was, I decided to read it out loud to Kathy. She said, "You need to email that to our daughters who think we raised them like that. Remind them that I let them be in the school play and I let them do sports. I never expected them to play the violin."

It was the first time I realized what driven parents we were. When our daughter Kristen was in Grade Eleven, she took on the "grumpy teenage girl" demeanour. Maybe she was just in that awkward phase that all teens go through from age twelve to about age... thirty-seven! I sat her down and told her that her attitude was unacceptable and that we expected her to be civil to her siblings and to us. She began to cry and said, "Do you expect me to be an A-student, a star athlete AND be nice!" Kathy and I both cracked up laughing and that just made her cry all the more. Now she will be mad that I mentioned it in this book.

Not all kids are going to excel in academics, or music, or sports, or drama, but they all bring a unique gifting into this world that we need to recognize and carefully nurture.

Chua's book is an interesting read, as she contrasts the difference between Eastern parenting and Western parenting. She is married to a Jewish white man from South Dakota, so she has witnessed both firsthand. She talks about how Western parents will carefully "tiptoe around" the perceived fragile psyches of their children, always worrying about never

---

75   Ibid.

putting too much pressure on them as to crush their self-esteem. By contrast, Chinese parents will expect perfection from their children and will shame them if they don't get it. One gets the impression that much of what she writes she believes, but some of it is clearly written tongue in cheek to make the point. For example,

> The fact is that Chinese parents can do things that would seem unimaginable—even legally actionable—to Westerners. Chinese mothers can say to their daughters, "Hey fatty—lose some weight." By contrast, Western parents have to tiptoe around the issue, talking in terms of "health" and never ever mentioning the f-word, and their kids still end up in therapy for eating disorders and negative self-image.[76]

Truth be told, the Hebrew parents of biblical times probably looked more like Chua's stereotypical Easterners. Consider the parenting instruction of Solomon's first few proverbs alone.

Hear, my children, the instruction of a father,
And give attention to know understanding...

—Proverbs 4:1

Therefore hear me now, my children,
And do not depart from the words of my mouth.

—Proverbs 5:7

Now therefore, listen to me, my children;
Pay attention to the words of my mouth...

—Proverbs 7:24

Now therefore, listen to me, my children,
For blessed are those who keep my ways.

—Proverbs 8:32

---

[76] Amy Chua, Battle Hymn of the Tiger Mother (New York: Penguin Books, 2011), p. 58.

The ideal parenting model probably lies somewhere between the extremes of Eastern and Western stereotypes. We also need to carefully adjust our approach based on the disposition of the child. Some kids do very well with hard and fast expectations, others do not.

Our own three kids are a perfect example of this. Our oldest two thrived on challenge and incentivized goals. I would offer monetary rewards for achieving the highest grades in a subject, and on school year-end Awards Night they always went home with a stack of cash. (For the record, Kathy and I did not agree with this approach, and she used to tell me I was teaching them to accept bribes. I argued that there was a big difference between bribes and rewards.) At any rate, it did not work in the least with our youngest. I would tell her at the beginning of the year that I would give her ten dollars for every highest mark. She would roll her eyes and say, "Oh, ten whole dollars! Who gives a rip?"

At the end of the school year on Awards Night, she would turn to me and say, "Oh, by the way, don't be expecting any top marks awards because it ain't gonna happen."

Hiding my disappointment, I would say, "Great, then I don't need to bother stopping at the bank for any cash." True to her word, she managed to get all the way through twelve years of school without ever winning a highest mark award. However, in her final high school year at the big Graduation Awards Night, we got a bit of a surprise. The night had unfolded as expected and she successfully managed not to win any high mark awards, but just before the final award of the night, one of the teachers seated behind me leaned forward and whispered in my ear, "This is the big one." The award was the somewhat humbly named Leadership Award and was presented to the student that had exemplified Christian leadership and made the biggest contribution in inspiring the rest of the student body during the Senior High School year. Imagine our surprise and joy when they called our daughter's name.

It was a great lesson for me. As highly intelligent as she was, she was never going to be motivated by rewards or by shame. She marches to the beat of her own drum, which is what makes her a leader. Today, this daughter is a licensed minister and works for me in our church with singles and young people. She routinely speaks in front of thousands of people with confidence and care. Her calling was not academics but leadership, and it took her and us a bit of time to figure that out. Not all kids are going to excel in academics, or music, or sports, or drama, but they all bring a unique gifting into this world that we need to recognize and carefully nurture.

Raising all our children to become doctors or professionals is not the goal, of course. The goal is to raise kids to pursue their passions and make a difference in this world. Reminding our offspring that they have been put on this earth for a purpose is the most important thing for them to understand.

In a country like Canada, which by most measurements would be considered a post-Christian secular nation, we as Christians have largely lost our moral voice. This is at least in part because we have not properly communicated to our Christian children that they have a mission to bring their influence to the table. C. S. Lewis once said, "The world does not need more Christian literature. What it needs is more Christians writing good literature," and this, "What we want is not more little books about Christianity, but more little books by Christians on other subjects—with their Christianity latent."[77] What he was saying is that Christians need to bring their faith into the marketplace in every endeavour. What the world needs is Christian lawyers, judges, politicians, doctors, professors, journalists, playwrights, artists, song writers, athletes, business leaders, and every career under the sun with our Christianity latent and making a difference.

4. STAYING VIGILANT

One day I received a letter in the mail from a sweet lady. She was writing for advice about her sons. She wrote, "Dear Pastor Mark, I do not know what to do with my boys. They will not come to church, they stay up all

---

[77] C. S. Lewis, *God in the Dock: Essays on Theology and Ethics*, ed. Walter Hooper (Grand Rapids, MI: William B. Eerdmans Publishing Company, 2014), p. 93.

night drinking and they get into trouble all over town. What should I do? By the way, my sons are sixty-five and sixty-seven, and I am ninety-two."

Those little rascals!

Notwithstanding her grief, it was hard not to be amused. Parenting is not for the faint of heart and it does not matter how old you are, you continue to carry the burden.

God has no grandchildren, only children. Every emerging generation has to find a personal relationship with Christ; just because we have, it does not mean that our children will. One of our greatest tasks as parents is to ensure that, above all else, we give our children every opportunity to find a personal relationship with Christ for themselves.

Before there was a Billy Graham there was a Billy Sunday, a fiery preacher who was saved while he was a famous major league baseball player. (Sunday had one season where he stole a record ninety-two bases.) In 1890, he left the outfield of the Philadelphia Phillies to become one of the most effective evangelists of his day. At the end of his life, however, he said that his greatest regret was that he saw tens of thousands of people come to Christ but lost his own children. Two sons died prematurely— one of multiple sclerosis and the other committed suicide. His third son lived a life of sexual immorality and drunkenness.[78]

These tragedies were avoidable mistakes. We can never assume that if we are doing God's work, He will take care of our kids. Taking care of our kids is doing God's work. Clergy or layman, our first and foremost mission field is always to our family. None of us need to lose our children to the world. God's promises say otherwise.

Research shows that a shocking sixty-six percent of young adults between the ages of eighteen and twenty-two years old will drop out of church.[79] We often hear this discouraging statistic when the subject of youth ministry comes up in churches. But we also need to hear that the

---

[78] Jack Wellman, "Who Was Billy Sunday?," Christian Crier (Patheos, June 16, 2016), http://www.patheos.com/blogs/christiancrier/2016/06/15/who-was-billy-sunday.

[79] Aaron Earls, "Most Teenagers Drop Out of Church as Young Adults," January 15, 2019, https://lifewayresearch.com/2019/01/15/most-teenagers-drop-out-of-church-as-young-adults.

same research has found that an encouraging two-thirds of them will eventually return to church at least sporadically.[80]

We have seen it many times. Young people who have gone off to chase after the bankrupt values of the world mostly end up married with children of their own. They look at these fragile little creatures and realize that they do not want them making the same stupid mistakes they made growing up. They do not want to see them smoking dope behind the 7-Eleven® or getting pregnant at fourteen. Many of them start to realize that the biggest positive influence they had in their lives was from godly Christian parents who took them to a Bible-based church. There is now virtually nowhere else in our culture where traditional moral values are still being taught. You will not find it in the daycares, schools, kids clubs, universities, movies, TV shows or virtually anywhere else. The church, and only the church, is the last bastion of upholding biblical values. These young families are recognizing that fact and wandering back into the church. It is an encouraging trend.

We know hundreds of parents who are praying that their children, who have gone astray, will return to their faith. We are all encouraged by parable of the Prodigal Son. The wayward son returns and the ever-forgiving father welcomes him back with open arms—what could be better? Well, if he never went astray in the first place, that's what would be better! The greatest trophies of grace are the ones who never departed from the faith, never began melting their brains on drugs and alcohol, never discarded their virginity like an old rag, never made mistakes that they will have to live with for the rest of their life.

As mentioned, the dropout rate of young people from the church today is at historic levels. There are many reasons for this, not the least being the aforementioned peer orientation; they are worried about missing out on all "the world" has to offer, the proverbial sex and drugs and rock and roll. However, parents bear a big responsibility in this as well.

For example, when we ask a young family to get involved with the church we will often hear, "I just don't have time; my family is my first priority." What they are really saying is that their primary interest is in

---

[80] Ibid.

their son's Sunday morning hockey. Unfortunately, Sunday morning has become the big day for sports, as it does not interfere with school and work. So, every week, Dad and Junior are down at the rink. This is not to say that Little Johnny's hockey is an unimportant part of his life, only that, maybe, it is esteemed too highly. Many boys develop a passion for the sport; we're Canadians, after all! The problem is that when any passion becomes an idol in our children's lives, to the exclusion of all else, we run the real risk of losing them to the faith. We have seen it too many times to count. In the end, after the years of investment, Little Johnny doesn't actually make it into the NHL, few do. No doubt, he learned some valuable lessons in discipline, commitment and how to handle disappointments in life, but he also missed out on church life and now has no interest in it as a young adult because it was not a valued part of his childhood. Why would it be? His parents sent him a message that his sports were more important than anything else. The whole family has been out of church for so long that usually none of them are involved any longer.

There are few things that will ever bring as much satisfaction and fulfillment as bringing children into the world and doing our best, as God enables, to raise the leaders of the next generation.

Here is the other one we pastors hear all the time: "Well, my kids just won't come to church… I can't make them come, can I?"

I answer their question with a question: "If there was a family birthday, would you expect your kids to attend? Or if it was Mother's Day, and you were taking Mom out for dinner, would they be expected to come? Why is this any different?" When our children live under our roof, they have—or should have—certain expectations of being part of a family.

We never "made" our kids come to church, but we did let them know that, as long as they were going to live under our roof, this was one of the things we were all going to do together. One of the benefits of a large church like ours is that we have multiple services on a weekend, including

Saturday night. Our children were all high performance athletes. Though none played hockey, they were highly involved in soccer, volleyball, track and pretty much every other sport. We supported them one hundred percent in their particular sports. However, they knew that sometime over the course of the weekend they were going to be in church, if not Sunday morning, then Saturday night. It was a non-negotiable part of being a member of our family. It was never once called into question by our kids because they understood the social contract that worked both ways.

We supported them in every endeavour: their sports, music, drama, hobbies, and education. We paid for half their university fees as well as let them live at home free of charge. We expected them to be involved in what was important to us as well. Consequently, we never had to twist their arms to attend church with us and they often thank us for giving them such a wonderful upbringing. Today, they are all adults living on their own and they are setting the stage to raise their own children the same way. All three of them are leaders in the church today and the greatest miracle of them all is they all still love to come and hear their dad preach. When I look back at my life, I am grateful for the level of success that God has given me in ministry, but by far, my greatest sense of accomplishment is that I have children that love Jesus and serve God. That is without question my greatest joy in life!

Notwithstanding the immense challenges of modern parenting, it is still one of life's greatest joys. There are few things that will ever bring as much satisfaction and fulfillment as bringing children into the world and doing our best, as God enables, to raise the leaders of the next generation. Our role as passionate parents runs from cradle to grave—their cradle, our grave. As long as we still have breath in our lungs, we are the parents, and God has given us all the tools within His Word to succeed at the task.

Chapter Fourteen

One for the Money

Money is not the most important thing in the world. Love is. Fortunately, I love money.

—Jackie Mason

Jesus talked more about money than any subject other than the Kingdom of God. That is because it is profoundly problematic. There are few things in life that are more difficult to bring into balance than money. It is spoken of in Scripture as both a blessing and a curse. Nothing in life has as much potential to do good or to do evil. Even the best among us struggle to manage the contradictions it creates.

You cannot live without money, and yet, if you find yourself wanting too much of it, it begins to control you instead of you controlling it. And the line is blurry where we cross into the "loving it too much" territory. That's because it is not a quantitative line but more of a qualitative one. It is really a matter of the heart. Money is not the sin, it is the love of money that is sinful. There were people in the Bible who God continued to bless financially even though they already had more than they could possibly ever need.

Then Isaac sowed in that land, and reaped in the same year a hundredfold; and the Lord blessed him. The man began to prosper, and continued prospering until he became very prosperous; for he had possessions of flocks and possessions of herds and a great number of servants. So the Philistines envied him.

—Genesis 26:12–14

This passage clearly states that the Lord was responsible for Isaac's extraordinary wealth, so it could not have been sinful for him to be wealthy. With examples like that, who could ever think that maybe they have too much wealth?

I have not yet met a single person who believes that they have too much money. I was visiting a very successful businessman one day, in his multimillion-dollar home. I could tell as he gave me, his pastor, a tour, that he felt uneasy about living like he did. Wanting to justify his lavish choices, he explained, "I know the house seems like a bit much, but I felt like the Lord told me that my wife deserved a home like this." Well, there you go. Who can argue with the Lord? I know that sounds a bit judgy on my part, but I also know that we all have an infinite capacity of self-justification.

Not unlike Jesus' teachings, the writings of King Solomon also talk more about money than just about any other subject. No examination of the life and times Solomon would be complete without digging into his considerable wisdom on the subject. I will warn you in advance, though, that there is a great incongruence between what he taught and how he lived. To say that he lived large would be a colossal understatement. His palace would make Windsor Castle look like it belonged in a trailer park. He was the wealthiest man of his time, possibly of any time. Some have estimated his wealth in today's dollars at one hundred billion dollars.[81] If that is the case, if he was alive today he would likely be the richest man on the planet, challenging the likes of Jeff Bezos, Bill Gates and Warren Buffet. At the very least, with the current price of gold he would have received a billion dollars a year in taxation income.

Each year Solomon received about 25 tons of gold. This did not include the additional revenue he received from merchants and traders. All the kings of Arabia and the governors of the provinces also brought gold and silver to Solomon…. So King Solomon became richer and wiser than any other king on earth. Kings from every nation came to consult him and to hear the wisdom God had given him. Year after year everyone who visited

---

81   Startupback.com team, "King Solomon Net Worth - How Much Was He Worth?" Startupback, May 24, 2020, https://startupback.com/king-solomon-wealth-net-worth.

brought him gifts of silver and gold, clothing, weapons, spices, horses, and mules. Solomon had 4,000 stalls for his horses and chariots and he had 12,000 horses. He stationed some of them in the chariot cities, and some near him in Jerusalem.

—2 Chronicles 9:13–14, 21– 25 NLT

It's hard to know what to make of all this. God promised to make him wealthy (1 Kings 3:13), but God also warned that the kings of Israel were not to multiply horses, chariots and gold for themselves.

But he shall not multiply horses for himself, nor cause the people to return to Egypt to multiply horses, for the Lord has said to you, "You shall not return that way again." Neither shall he multiply wives for himself, lest his heart turn away; nor shall he greatly multiply silver and gold for himself.

—Deuteronomy 17:16–17

King Solomon was clearly in contravention of the established rules for kingship. It is hard to miss the irony here. On the one hand, we read all about Solomon's excessive wealth, and on the other hand, he doles out dire warnings for those that place too high a value on becoming rich.

Do not overwork to be rich; Because of your own understanding, cease!

—Proverbs 23:4

A faithful man will abound with blessings, But he who hastens to be rich will not go unpunished.

—Proverbs 28:20

Seriously, Solomon? So, it's OK for you to have your opulence and mega-wealth but you want to relegate the rest of us to being content with integrity and simple blessings? What is that all about?

It would seem the world's most passionate man did everything to excess and was often blind to his own folly.

> Most of us have experienced how wealth has a way of bringing out the worst in people. We all know individuals who were better people when they were poor than when they were rich.

Of all the corrupt passions of fallen mankind, none are as powerful as the love of money. People will steal, cheat, lie and kill for money. Even otherwise honest people will find themselves lying or cheating on their income tax to save a few bucks. It is the only human passion that the Bible places on the level of deity.

"No servant can serve two masters; for either he will hate the one and love the other, or else he will be loyal to the one and despise the other. You cannot serve God and Mammon." Now the Pharisees, who were lovers of money, also heard all these things, and they derided Him.
—Luke 16:13–14

In this passage, Jesus carefully uses the word *mammon* instead of *money*. Money in and of itself could be regarded as nothing more than a means of exchange. Mammon was an Aramaic term that meant "riches" or "wealth." The lexicographer J. Thayer describes it as "the treasure a person trusts in." Jesus personifies mammon and puts it on the level of a deity in opposition to God. He claimed that people have to decide if they were going to serve God or mammon. It turns out that our modern expression "The Almighty Dollar" is quite appropriate.

One of my good childhood friends ended up becoming the CEO of his father's very successful company. They have revenues of some two hundred million dollars every year. They had so much money they didn't know what to do with it all, so they started buying up all the properties around their business. One parcel was located right next to our church building. We were short of parking, so I gave him a call. One of the great things about old friends is you can talk straight and don't have to beat around the bush. I said, "Listen, Greg, you have that land sitting doing nothing and we need more parking. I have a great idea—why don't you give it to us?"

After he finished laughing, I explained to him that he could get a tax receipt for the donation and it would be a great way to deal with the tax problem he probably had from making too much money. After he laughed a second time, I suggested that maybe this was fate's way of giving him a way to make a contribution back to the community that had been so good to him. He laughed yet a third time, saying, "That will never happen." I asked him why not, and this time without laughing he explained, "Mark, haven't you figured out that I worship the Almighty Dollar?"

"Yes, I do know that." I responded without hesitation, "That's why I was giving you this opportunity to redeem yourself." He laughed yet again.

We were not exactly seeing eye to eye, but at least we were having a good laugh. We spent some time catching up on old times and I said I would take a run at him again another time. He said he looked forward to it and we said goodbye. It was an idle threat and I never did follow up, as I knew the deal was not going to happen.

Most of us have experienced how wealth has a way of bringing out the worst in people. We all know individuals who were better people when they were poor than when they were rich. Solomon put it this way, *"The poor man uses entreaties, But the rich answers roughly"* (Proverbs 18:23).

Money has a way of making us feel superior to those who do not have it. I remember years ago being asked by my senior pastor to chauffeur around a well-known visiting guest preacher. He had arrived in our city in his ministry's personal jet, which is not something we ever see in Canada. He had arrived hungry and wanted to stop for a bite to eat. (I guess even personal jets no longer serve in-flight meals.) At the restaurant he treated the waitress like dirt when she brought out the wrong type of bread for his toast. "It's not rocket science, sweetheart, it's just a piece of toast!" he said, among other things. I was so embarrassed that, after we had left, I told him I had forgotten something in the restaurant and went back in. It was really him who had forgotten something—his human decency. I apologized to the waitress and told her that my friend was just cranky because he was off his meds and out on a weekend pass. She laughed and I gave her a generous tip. Again, Solomon called it when he said, *"Better is the poor who walks in his integrity Than one perverse in his ways, though he be rich"* (Proverbs 28:6).

People with money almost always think they are smarter than people without it. Solomon put it this way: *"The rich man is wise in his own eyes, But the poor who has understanding searches him out"* (Proverbs 28:11).

When we were growing up, behind his downstairs wet bar my father had a poster of two hobos standing in a back alley. The one was saying to the other, "If you're so darn smart, why ain't you rich?" It is funny how we like to make that association. It is very unbecoming and yet we see it all the time. The rich start to believe their own press that if they have money, then they must also have good judgement. It is about then that they start to make poor decisions because they have become snared in their own pride.

At the risk of touching on the polarizing world of American politics, I was always amused by Donald Trump's claim something to the effect that he was "very, very smart" because he "very, very rich."[82] Or maybe it was the other way around. At any rate, he felt the combination was what qualified him to be President. Maybe he is rich, and maybe he is smart, but my contention is that the two are never considered synonymous. It is possible to be rich and not smart, or smart and not rich.

All these characteristics of what money does to people are pretty damnable. History has shown repeatedly that the rich will oppress the poor to gain more wealth. The rich not only feel fully deserving of their wealth, but they will justify any means to gain it.

The feudal land systems of the past were designed to allow the rich to become richer and the poor to become poorer. Today in the West, we have it better than ever with the advent of a middle class (which we will look at in the next chapter), but we still seem to get the short end of the stick, with millionaires and billionaires paying less tax than we do. It is because the rich control the socioeconomics, regardless of the type of

---

[82]   Cody Cain, "Presidential Debate: Donald Trump's Wealth Is Fool's Gold," Time.com (*Time*, October 7, 2016), https://time.com/4521851/donald-trumps-wealth.

political system a nation might have. The ultra-rich will always be able to buy big tax breaks from the politicians they own.

The average Joe is encouraged to save for retirement by investing in a stock market that is manipulated by trading robots and hedge funds. Though many have done well with their investments, it is hard to trust the powers behind this beast that doesn't do anything for the benefit of others. I got a kick out of how *Forbes* magazine's Matt Taibbi put it:

> The world's most powerful investment bank is a great vampire squid wrapped around the face of humanity, relentlessly jamming its blood funnel into anything that smells like money.[83]

The economic meltdown of 2008 was entirely manmade by a subprime mortgage scheme that sold worthless, bundled mortgages to unsuspecting investors. When the bubble burst, families lost their homes, investors lost their pensions and the very investment bankers that created the fiasco, Bear Stearns, Merrill Lynch, JP Morgan and public enemy number one, the giant vampire squid Goldman Sacks, received billions of dollars in bailouts from the US government. They did not reimburse their suffering clients but took those bailout dollars and bought up depressed stocks at bargain basement prices and drove the market to new heights, making them more untold billions. What they did was downright criminal, yet they congratulated themselves for pulling America from the brink of disaster.

I realize I sound like a raving socialist when I talk like this, but I assure you I am just a realist. Every single political/economic system is fundamentally flawed because the people in the systems are flawed. Sinful people abuse power for their own gain. Having said that, some systems are better than others.

Here's the illustration that best explains economic theory; it is called The Two Cows Political Theory of Economics. It goes like this:

---

[83] Jake Zamansky, "The Great Vampire Squid Keeps On Sucking" (*Forbes*, August 8, 2013), https://www.forbes.com/sites/jakezamansky/2013/08/08/the-great-vampire-squid-keeps-on-sucking/#2db4d2e27df8.

- **Socialism**: You have two cows. The government takes one and gives it to your lazy neighbor.

- **Communism**: You have two cows. The government takes both and gives you some milk.

- **Fascism**: You have two cows. The government takes both sells you some milk.

- **Bureaucracy**: You have two cows. The government takes both, shoots one, milks other, and throws away the milk.

- **Nazism**: You have two cows. The government takes both and shoots you.

- **Capitalism**: You have two cows. You sell one and buy a bull.

Speaking of cows, the Alberta Department of Labour got a tip that a local rancher was not paying proper wages to his employees. They sent an investigator out to his Leduc ranch. "I need a list of your employees and how much you pay them," the investigator told the rancher.

"Well," replied the rancher, "there's my ranch hand who's been with me for five years. I pay him $1,200 a week plus free room and board. The cook has been here for two years, and I pay her one thousand dollars per week plus free room and board. Then there's the half-wit. He works about eighteen hours every day and does about ninety percent of all the work around here. He makes about one hundred dollars per week and pays his own room and board. But I buy him a case of beer every Saturday night and he sleeps with the wife on occasion."

"That's the guy I want to talk to… the half-wit!" says the investigator.

"Well, start talking," replied the rancher, "because that would be me."

Ok, yes, this chapter sort of "railed against the man," but unless we understand the dangers of mammon we are doomed before we start. There are just so many pitfalls along the way.

These next chapters, however, will look at the timeless principles of financial success that King Solomon left behind for the generations that would follow. Industrious and hardworking people who apply these principles judiciously will reap extraordinary rewards.

Chapter Fifteen

The Daily Grind

For the love of money is the root of all evil.

—Saint Paul

The lack of money is the root of all evil.

—Mark Twain

Notwithstanding all his warnings about the evils of money, some of Solomon's best writings help us learn how to increase in wealth. Let's face it, most of us we will never have to worry about the burden of having too much money, as we are too busy struggling along without enough of it. Motivational speaker Zig Ziglar put it this way: *"Money isn't the most important thing in life, but it's reasonably close to oxygen on the 'gotta have it' scale."*[84]

Being born to be king and being the smartest man in the world gave Solomon certain clear advantages. Fortunately for us, he wrote down his secrets to financial success as well as his warnings. Because the Proverbs are short and pithy, they sometimes don't look like much. It is easy to miss the powerful truths. Lying within these short verses of prose are understated principles of success that are capable of exponentially increasing our ability to generate wealth.

---

[84]   Zig Ziglar, "Money isn't the most important thing," Facebook, April 13, 2013, 3:25 p.m., https://www.facebook.com/ZigZiglar/posts/money-isnt-the-most-important-thing-in-life-but-its-reasonably-close-to-oxygen-o/10151543396792863.

We will look at just three of these proverbs over the next three chapters, which, in my own proverbial way, I prescribe as Grind It Out, Get Good at It and Give It Away.

1. Grind It Out

The soul of a lazy man desires, and has nothing;
But the soul of the diligent shall be made rich.

—Proverbs 13:4

The baseball story of Cal Ripken Jr. is the story of an unassuming success. If you asked any real baseball fan what Ripken was best known for, they would all say the same thing—"showing up for work." No kidding; that is his claim to fame. He played for the Baltimore Orioles for twenty-one seasons. He holds the record for playing the most consecutive games in Major League Baseball. At 2,632 games in a row, it is doubtful that anyone will ever surpass him. He grew up in a baseball family, in that his father, Cal Ripken Sr., was a coach with the Oriole organization. As one of the hardest working players in baseball, Cal Jr. was drafted by his hometown team and played his entire career with them. Year after year, game after game, he showed up and gave his best effort every time.

If you do something long enough and consistently enough, you will get good at it. And whatever that something is, someone will pay you to do it.

When fans of the game were asked to vote on the "most memorable moment" in the history of the game, they picked September 6, 1995. On that day, the Orioles were playing the Angels and in the fifth inning it was official: Cal Ripken Jr. had just surpassed Lou Gehrig's record of 2,130 games. The Baltimore crowd rose to their feet and gave him a standing ovation for a full twenty-two minutes. Being the quiet and unassuming man that he was, he had to be pushed out of the dugout to take a victory lap. Finally, they had to ask the crowd to stop so that the game could continue. As if scripted and on cue, Ripken had already stepped up to the plate and hit a home run.

Even though that moment was his idiomatic "fifteen minutes of fame," it was what he did, day after day, that made him a superstar. His work ethic was second to none in baseball, and as result, over his twenty-one years with the Orioles, Ripken compiled 3,184 hits, 431 home runs, and 1,695 runs batted in. He won two Gold Glove Awards for defense. He was a nineteen-time All-Star and was twice named the American League's Most Valuable Player. He is one of only seven men who have hit more than four hundred home runs. His name is listed in the National Baseball Hall of Fame alongside the likes of Babe Ruth and Mickey Mantle.

If you do something long enough and consistently enough, you will get good at it. And whatever that something is, someone will pay you to do it. Today, Ripken's net worth is estimated at seventy-five million dollars. Not bad for a six foot, four inch short stop with a passion for baseball.

> The price of success is hard work, dedication to the job at hand, and the determination that whether we win or lose, we have applied the best of ourselves to the task at hand.
>
> —Vince Lombardi

Passionate people succeed in life because they work hard. When you love what you do and are passionate about it, it is not a challenge to put countless hours into your endeavour. These people never watch the clock, much less punch it. When you find passionate people, you find hardworking and prosperous people. They are the individuals that have come to love what they do and have applied themselves industriously. Generally—and there are always exceptions due to unforeseen circumstances—these people will prosper! Today, in countries like communist China, and even India, where the Hindu caste system would have formerly prevented a person from upward mobility, a new financial middle class has emerged as they move towards more free market economies. In affluent North America, there is little reason for a hardworking person to not be able to prosper.

For most of human history, the middle class did not even exist; there were just the rich and the poor. The rich were the kings or chiefs or feudal landowners who controlled most of the resources while the poor were subservient workers that slaved, often literally, to keep the landowner in the lap of luxury. If you ever get to Cairo, Egypt, and visit the great pyramids, it won't take you long to realize that the entire population would have had to work feverishly to keep the Pharaoh and his family in wealth, not only in this life but into the next. It is overwhelming even just looking at the Pyramids of Giza that soar some 455 feet into the heavens, each built so that one man and his worldly possessions could be buried and transported into the next life. The countless years of slavery and hard labour that must have been required is hard to imagine.

There were non-aristocratic individuals that prospered at certain points along the human timeline, but it wasn't until the Protestant Reformers came along that an entirely new class of people began to flourish. Sociologist Max Weber has done some of the most revealing work on this subject. He is usually credited for connecting the dots of the middle-class to the Protestantism. In his landmark 1905 book, *The Protestant Ethic and the Spirit of Capitalism*,[85] Weber observed that the work ethic of the reformed and anabaptist protestant churches taught their adherents the values of industriousness, hard work, and individualism. As Christian people applied these principles, they began to prosper and succeed in everything to which they set their hands. It is exactly what Solomon said would happen: *"the soul of the diligent shall be made rich"* (Proverbs 13:4). Diligence produces good results. Laziness produces results as well—bad results.

Solomon wrote his most sardonic stuff on the subject of laziness:

As a door turns on its hinges,
So does the lazy man on his bed.

—Proverbs 26:14

---

[85]   Max Weber, Anthony Giddens, and Talcott Parsons, *The Protestant Ethic and the Spirit of Capitalism* (London: Routledge, 2001), pp. 3-10.

The lazy man buries his hand in the bowl;
It wearies him to bring it back to his mouth.

—Proverbs 26:15

Because of laziness the building decays,
And through idleness of hands the house leaks.

—Ecclesiastes 10:18

We have a wonderful case study of the Protestant work ethic right here in southern Manitoba. We have many communities that were founded primarily by Mennonites. They were Anabaptist Christians who were originally followers of Dutch reformer Menno Simmons. As pacifists and conscientious objectors, they came to Canada in the late 1800s and early 1900s, fleeing compulsory Russian military service in Eastern Europe. As a result, most arrived with nothing.

Originally, the Mennonites were placed on rural "reservations," where they built homes, barns and, of course, a church. Their work ethic and ingenuity became readily apparent as they expanded their footprint all across southern Manitoba. They were the first farmers to build shelter belts around their properties to protect livestock from inclement weather. They were the first to introduce fruit trees and new crops like sunflowers to Western Canada. They built windmills and steam mills to grind wheat into flour for personal use and domestic markets. They were also the first to grow wheat on a large scale, leading to Manitoba becoming a net exporter of wheat only a few years after their arrival.[86] Today, as you drive across the province, you not only see their successful modern farm operations but their bustling, prosperous communities. I have known some families that struggled with the inner conflict of trying to maintain a level of modesty in the midst of their obvious financial affluence.

Years ago, I was a bit of a "motivational speaker" junkie. I read the books and watched the videos of people like Zig Ziglar, Dennis Waitley

---

[86] Victor Peters, "Manitoba and Its Mennonites," *Manitoba* 29, no. 6, 1974, Germans from Russia Heritage Collection (NDSU Libraries), accessed June 5, 2020, https://library.ndsu.edu/grhc/history_culture/history/mennonites.html.

and Norman Vincent Peale. I am sure people can see the residual effects of this even in my preaching today. There was one encounter from those days that will stick in my mind forever. It was the first and only time I ever saw the late Charlie "Tremendous" Jones. He got that nickname because he used the word "tremendous" in everything, including the title of his two-million-copy bestseller, *Life is Tremendous*.[87] His most enduring expression was that the only things that really change an individual are "the books we read and the people we meet." He probably would have known something about that, since he conducted over five thousand seminars and had a library of books that would be the envy of any collector. His personal collection included the only known complete set of Oswald Chamber's hardcovers, over 270 volumes on Abe Lincoln alone, eighty-five on George Washington, and countless others on David Livingston, General George Patton, Winston Churchill, etc.

During the seminar, Charlie said right at the outset that he was going to give us the most important success principle he had ever learned. He went on to explain how it would change and transform our lives. He told us to get pen and paper ready, then he told story after story about the results we would get, the whole while building anticipation as to what it might be. He asked us again and again if we thought we were ready to hear it. As an audience we got more animated, if not a little frustrated, with our affirmative. Finally, in the last five minutes of his talk, after much hype, he said, "Ok, here it is: if you want to succeed in life you need to WORK! WORK! WORK is the key to success. Nobody succeeds without work. If you want any chance whatsoever of achieving your goals in life, you have to work for them." Yes, it was good for a laugh and, for sure, a bit of a letdown. But I have never forgotten it!

To this day, I think it was some of the best advice I have ever heard. It demolishes any sense of entitlement that we might otherwise entertain. Nothing in life just comes to you. If you want a successful marriage, you have to work for it. If you want to be a good parent, you have to work at it. If you want to be a good Christian, you have to work at it. Whatever you

---

[87] Charles E. Jones, *Life Is Tremendous!* (Wheaton, IL: Tyndale House Publishers, 1981).

desire to achieve, you just work, and work hard for it. What did Solomon say? *"The soul of the diligent shall be made rich"* (Proverbs 13:4).

So, the first key to financial success is to simply *grind it out.* Work hard and good things will come your way. The second key is an inevitability of the first—if you *grind it out,* you will *get good at it.*

Chapter Sixteen

In Search of Excellence

Excellence is to do a common thing in an uncommon way.

—Booker T. Washington

2. Get Good at It

I never really followed automobile racing until Danica Patrick got into the game. To race car fans, she is a household name. The thing that piqued my interest was the fact that she had the same name as our youngest daughter, Danica.[88]

In fact, my Danica was once mistaken for the other Danica. A couple of years ago she was in the library, renewing her card. The librarian looked at her name and said, "I know you! I have seen you race."

To which my Danica said, "What?"

The woman pressed in, "You are a race car driver; I have seen you race."

To which Danica said, "Well, I do own a sports car."

Validated, the woman insisted, "I knew it! I have seen you race many times."

My daughter corrected her, "I think you might be thinking of Danica Patrick?"

"Nope", she insisted looking again at the library card, "I am thinking of you, Danica Hughes." At that my daughter checked out her book, *Formula One Racing by Mario Andretti*, and left confused.

---

[88]   We pronounce it the Slavic way, dah-nee-ka, which means "morning star," but Ms. Patrick pronounces her name dan-ika.

Danica Patrick came by her passion for auto racing honestly. Both her parents were gear heads and her father raced snowmobiles and motocross bikes as well as dabbling in midget cars. By the time Danica was ten, she was racing go-karts. She had an aptitude for the sport, and by age sixteen she dropped out of school and moved to England to race Formula Fords, which are entry-level open-wheel cars. As a consummate competitor, she would always push herself to become faster every race. She graduated through the ranks of open-wheel disciplines all the way up to Indy Cars.

At a towering five feet, two inches tall, one hundred pounds and only twenty-three years old, Danica Patrick became the fourth woman ever to qualify for the Indianapolis 500, finishing fourth and earning the title of Rookie of the Year in 2005. Some fellow competitors complained that she had an unfair advantage due to her comparatively low body weight.[89] Danica believes she has gotten where she has in life on her own merit, saying, "I've never asked for special treatment along the way. And I'm never going to hide the fact that I'm a girl, ever. That's obvious, isn't it?"[90]

In 2008, she became the first and only woman in history to win an Indy race, finishing number one in the Indy Japan 300. In 2011, she made the switch to NASCAR and finished sixth in her very first race. Her success as a racer has spilled over into many areas of her life, including acting on *CSI: NY*, modeling for Victoria Secret and several times being named to FHM's "100 Sexiest Women in the World." As a father, I am not sure what I would think of my daughter being one of the sexiest women in the world, but whatever! In her final years of racing, Danica was earning over ten million dollars a year.[91] In 2018, she disappointed her fans when she

---

[89]   Dave Caldwell, "As Patrick's Star Rises, I.R.L. Is Along for Ride" (*The New York Times*, May 31, 2005), http://www.nytimes.com/2005/05/31/sports/othersports/as-patricks-star-rises-irl-is-along-for-ride.html.

[90]   Rachel Ray, "Daytona 500: Racing Superstar Danica Patrick Commits Career to America's NASCAR," (*The Telegraph*, February 26, 2012), https://www.telegraph.co.uk/sport/motorsport/indycar/9106630/Daytona-500-Racing-superstar-Danica-Patrick-commits-career-to-Americas-NASCAR.html.

[91]   Michelle Kessel, John Kapetaneas, and Pavni Mittal, "Racing Star Danica Patrick Reflects on Her Career, Why She's Choosing to Retire: 'It Wasn't in My Heart Anymore'," ABC News (ABC News Network, May 25, 2018), https://abcnews.go.com/Lifestyle/racing-star-danica-patrick-reflects-career-shes-choosing/story?id=55443949.

announced her retirement from racing. When asked why she was leaving the sport, she replied, "I came to realize maybe racing wasn't my true passion anymore."[92]

Danica had always contended that "for anything to be successful, it needs to come from a place of passion"[93] She is a woman who rose to the top in a man's sport because she believed that it had nothing to do with her gender. She was fond of saying, "I was brought up to be the fastest driver, not the fastest girl."[94]

Jesus concluded His "Parable of the Talents" with these words: *"Well done, good and faithful servant; you have been faithful over a few things, I will make you ruler over many things. Enter into the joy of your lord"* (Matthew 25:23). He didn't say, "reasonably done," "fairly done" or "mediocrely done"—no, He said, "Well done!" Passionate people get good at what they do.

> *Do you see a man who excels in his work? He will stand before kings; He will not stand before unknown men.*
>
> —Proverbs 22:29

Daniel is one of the greatest heroes in all of Scripture. He is the subject of an entire book of the Bible and he is the only major character in the Old Testament without a single recorded mistake or moral failure. Daniel was only around twenty years old when King Nebuchadnezzar sacked Jerusalem and destroyed the city. He was one of the young men who were taken away as slaves to the capital of Babylon, and the first order of business for them was castration. (Ouch! Most people are unaware of this fact, but it's in the text: 2 Kings 20:18 and Daniel 1:9). Far from

---

[92] McKenna Moore, "Why Danica Patrick Planned for Retirement When She Started Racing" (*Fortune*, October 3, 2018), http://fortune.com/2018/10/02/danica-patrick-business-retirement.

[93] *Danica Patrick: 'For Anything to Be Successful, It Needs to Come From a Place of Passion'* (*Entrepreneur*, 2018), https://www.entrepreneur.com/video/324714.

[94] Associated Press, "Danica Patrick Wins Daytona Pole," ESPN (ESPN Internet Ventures, February 17, 2013), https://www.espn.com/racing/nascar/cup/story/_/id/8956961/danica-patrick-first-woman-win-daytona-500-pole.

feeling emasculated, Daniel adhered to the principles of the faith that he had been raised in, refusing to compromise on anything.

When they tried to fatten him up on the delicacies of the king's palace, where he lived, he refused. He was not going to scarf down escargot and frog's legs when the Torah had specifically forbidden them, so he made a deal with the chief of the eunuchs for himself and his friends Shadrach, Meshach, Abed-Nego—or as I like to call them, the three Jewish contractors: My Shack, Your Shack and A Bungalow. In order to allow them to prove they could look healthier in only ten days, he asked to eat only vegetables and drink no wine The experiment was a success and the four of them were allowed to carry on with their vegan diet indefinitely.

The entire story is a captivating and inspiring read, but there is one verse that should jump out at you as you go through the book.

> *Then this Daniel distinguished himself above the governors and satraps, because an excellent spirit was in him; and the king gave thought to setting him over the whole realm.*
>
> —Daniel 6:3

Daniel could have become distressed and dismayed when he was taken away as a slave. He could have thought that all his dreams as a young man were dashed because his circumstances would never allow him to be anything more than a defeated eunuch. Instead, he understood that his success in life had nothing to do with the limitations of his lot in life. In the midst of overwhelming odds, he demonstrated the spirit of excellence.

This idea of working and getting good at it is a profoundly simple truth that many people miss because they are looking for a shorter route to success.

How did a young man like Daniel have such clear understanding of such things? It was not an accident. Daniel was brought up to be a student of the Word of God. He would have read the letter that was sent from Jeremiah to the captives in Babylon. Jeremiah, under the inspiration of the Holy Spirit, warned the captives that they would not be coming home to Jerusalem any time soon and that they would be there for seventy years. This is how he told them to deal with their situation:

> *Thus says the Lord of hosts, the God of Israel, to all who were carried away captive, whom I have caused to be carried away from Jerusalem to Babylon: Build houses and dwell in them; plant gardens and eat their fruit. Take wives and beget sons and daughters; and take wives for your sons and give your daughters to husbands, so that they may bear sons and daughters—that you may be increased there, and not diminished. And seek the peace of the city where I have caused you to be carried away captive, and pray to the Lord for it; for in its peace you will have peace.*
>
> —Jeremiah 29:4–7

Well, Daniel would not be taking a wife any time soon, if you know what I mean, but the rest of his marching orders were clear. He would establish himself in his new home even if he was a captive. He knew that he was a child of the living God and the Lord was the only one Who could put limitations on his life. He was going to be a man of faith, dedication and hard work. He would continue to search for excellence, irrespective of the situation in which he found himself.

Even though he began his journey as a slave, not a king, like Solomon, Daniel determined that he was going to be the most faithful and valuable slave in the kingdom. From his lowly position he rose to become the ruler over the entire province of Babylon and chief administrator over all the wise men. Daniel then petitioned the king, and he set Shadrach, Meshach, and Abed-Nego as his lieutenants over the affairs of the province of Babylon as well (Daniel 2:48–49). He certainly did not choose his career path, but by challenging fate, he rose to become a "Jewish" leader of the very pagan kingdom that was an enemy of Israel. He dwelt his entire adult life in exile, seventy years in total, and never did go home to Jerusalem. Instead, Daniel outlived four different kings and endured the conquests of three different kingdoms—from the Babylonians to the Medes to the Persians—serving as a ruler in every single one of them. It is truly a remarkable story. I don't think any of us ever have a legitimate excuse when we say that we cannot get ahead in life because of our boss!

The story of Daniel should inspire every one of us to believe that we can excel in life regardless of where we start. Daniel was a captive but became the best slave he could be, rising far above what anyone would have thought possible. We don't need to be the best in the world, but we should strive to be the best we can be. We can't all be a Danica Patrick (especially if you are a guy), but that should not stop us from being the very best person we can be at what we do. We can still become the best bus driver we can be, the best cab driver, the best Uber driver, the best delivery driver, truck driver, the best ferry driver, the best forklift driver or the best pile driver. We should never look at our lot in life and conclude that we are somehow limited.

This idea of working and getting good at it is a profoundly simple truth that many people miss because they are looking for a shorter route to success; when it does not come forthwith, they quit and do something else. The average North American will now have twelve to fifteen different jobs in their life. There is nothing wrong with trying to find the right passion in life—that is what this book is about—but when we are constantly changing paths we are continually starting over. It is hard to get good at something if we perennially find ourselves at the bottom, beginning again.

Thomas Edison was famous for saying, "Genius is 1% inspiration, and 99% perspiration." We should not imagine him as a reclusive inventor tweaking the light bulb in a candle-lit basement. He held 1,093 patents and was a hugely successful industrialist who owned and operated entire factories. He is credited for inventing both the concept of mass production and the research laboratory. He was a friend and partner with Henry Ford and the two of them transformed the North American economy through their innovations. Edison's basic philosophy of work was that while most men spent their sixteen waking hours on many different things, he focused on only one singular thing until he perfected it.[95] He was so obsessive about mastering every challenge that he refused to have a clock in his office, but he did have a bed. He did not care what time of day or night it was. If he ran out of gas, he would catch a couple hours of sleep and carry on. There is no doubt that he would have lived a life totally out of balance, and I am sure he was a terrible husband and father. He was married twice and had six children, but nobody ever talks about that. I wonder why? He did, however, know how to grind it out and get good at it.

My childhood friend, Neil, was the black sheep of his family. His father was a very accomplished doctor and they grew up with all the privileges of an upper middle-class family: a beautiful home, a summer cottage, winter ski vacations, cars and boats… the whole nine yards. They socialized with other doctors, lawyers, politicians, businesspeople, and the like. Neil never really fit in with that crowd. His father tried to instill the virtues of higher education every chance he got, but Neil did poorly at school. His teachers requested a hearing test every year, assuming he must be deaf because he never knew what was going on and spent the whole day looking out the window, waiting for recess. Turned out his hearing was perfect—he just wasn't too bright… or at least, that's what everybody thought. Neil managed to finish high school and went to work in a local factory. His father would explain his son to everybody by saying, apologetically, "At least he has a job."

Neil, however, excelled on the factory floor and they soon discovered that he was very good with his hands and could fix anything. This came from his childhood interest in anything with a motor: snowmobiles, boats, motorcycles, etc. They trained Neil as a power engineer and he worked at maintaining all the mechanical equipment. He got very good at it and eventually he headed up the whole department. By the time he was only fifty years old, he was making a very handsome income. At this point the company was bought out and the new owners decided to retire off

---

[95]   Orison Swett Marden, *How They Succeeded: Life Stories of Successful Men and Women Told by Themselves*, retrieved July 22, 2020, from Mises Institute, https://cdn.mises.org/How%20They%20Succeeded%20Life%20Stories%20of%20Successful%20Men%20and%20Women%20Told%20by%20Themselves_2.pdf, p. 237.

the old guard. Neil got a buy out and a full pension, but then they turned around and hired him back on a consultant basis. He was making as much as before and collecting his pension on top of that.

Today he lives in a million-dollar lake house and has a fully equipped mechanics shop out back full of snowmobiles, motorcycles and boats. He spends the winter down south racing moto-cross and the rest of the year consulting with his former employers. When he was growing up, no one would have ever guessed that Neil would become the most financially successful of all his siblings. He would have made a terrible doctor or lawyer, but he found his lane in life and excelled in it.

When people find their purpose and their passion in life, they work hard at it, and getting good at it will naturally follow. And when you are good at something, someone will pay you to do it.

Unfortunately, it is not uncommon to see people in lifelong careers who no longer have their passion. They have been in coast mode for years. They are perhaps decent at what they do but could almost literally do it in their sleep.

Why would anyone go through life being content with mediocrity? We were created for excellence. We should wake up every morning with a desire that, by the end of the day, we will have learned something, accomplished something or improved something.

As a young preacher, the first book I studied thoroughly from beginning to end was the book of Daniel. I remember thinking I wanted to model my life after him and strive for the same faithfulness and excellence he exhibited. It didn't matter that it would be next to impossible; I could commit my life to giving it my best shot. After over thirty years of preaching, I still try to approach every single sermon with the goal that it will be better than the last. "Well, you sure can't tell!" Yeah, yeah, I know. I said *I try*, not *I succeed*. Nevertheless, because I have done the same thing for so long, I have become reasonably good at it. I am still surprised that people will pay me to talk. Most people do their talking for free. And there are some that should have to pay to make others listen to them.

I can't help but think of the story of the three young boys in the playground boasting about what their fathers do for a living. The first one says, "My father is a poet. He scribbles a few words on a piece of paper, calls it a poem and they pay him fifty dollars for it." The second says, "My father is a songwriter. He scribbles a few words on a piece of paper, calls it a song and they pay him one hundred dollars for it." The third one says, "My father is a pastor. He scribbles a few words on a piece of paper, calls it a sermon and it takes eight men with buckets to collect all the money."

Success in life is not just from working hard but also from getting good at what we do along the way. It almost doesn't matter what we do—if we will keep doing it, we will get good at it, and if we get good at it, people will pay us to do it. *Grind it out, get good at it...* and the last of Solomon's simple success principles is to *give it away.*

Chapter Seventeen

The Brim Reaper

No one has ever become poor by giving.

—Anne Frank

3. Give it Away

Giving is God's supernatural means of creating wealth. It is so counterintuitive that many people, even some Christians, never figure it out. How could giving away what you already have possibly lead to a greater abundance?

It is called the Law of *Sowing and Reaping*. Every farmer understands this principle and would be out of business if they didn't. Each spring they must take some of their hard-earned crop from the year before and donate it back to the earth from whence it came. They will never get that seed back, but that seed has the power to recreate itself multiple times.

Jesus employed this metaphor several times, even referring to the multiples of thirty-, sixty- and one-hundred-fold (Matthew 13:23). These are interesting numbers since, depending on the crop, it might be exactly what you could expect as a return. Canola might return thirty-fold; wheat, sixty-fold; and corn, one-hundred-fold (although, with modern farming practices the numbers are now increasing dramatically). When we invest in the world's economy, we are thrilled if we can find a ten percent annual return on our investment. A hundredfold is ten thousand percent. It doesn't even seem possible. It must be a scam, right?

Luke 6:38 says, *"Give, and it will be given to you: good measure, pressed down, shaken together, and running over will be put into your bosom. For with the same measure that you use, it will be measured back to you."* This verse tells us that when we sow it will come back to us in an overflowing way. "Your cup runneth over," so to speak, and hence, the chapter title name: "The Brim Reaper." This verse is not speaking exclusively about money but about everything in life. Anything we give away will come back to us. If you love someone, they will usually love you back. When you smile at someone, they will almost always smile back. If you complement someone, they will often complement you right back. It is a fantastic principle that is one of life's true joys.

Passionate people overflow. They are contagious on every level and want to share what they have with others.

To be clear, the corollary also exists. If you scowl at someone, they scowl back. If you criticize someone, you had better brace yourself for a nasty harvest because it could come back to you thirty-, sixty- or one-hundred-fold. The apostle Paul put it even more specifically when he said, *"Do not be deceived, God is not mocked; for whatever a man sows, that he will also reap"* (Galatians 6:7). Whatever means *whatever*! This concept of sowing and reaping is the basis for the heavenly economy here on earth. The idea of *working hard* and *getting good at it* will get you only so far in most cases, but *giving it away* is the catalyst for truly extraordinary results.

> *There is one who scatters, yet increases more; And there is one who with-holds more than is right, But it leads to poverty.*
> —Proverbs 11:24

Years ago, when I was a young man, I had a friend in our church who had decided to accept the call to the mission field in Guatemala. Doug was a passionate believer and there was nothing he would not do if God asked him to. He did not have much to his name, and instead of selling off his few worldly possessions, he decided to just give it all away before he left.

The only thing he had of any real value was his rusted-up Toyota Corolla. He gave it away to a single mom in the church. It was a generous move, but it sort of made me mad at him, as I thought it was more reasonable to sell it and raise some funds for his new adventure. Doug said, "Hey, if you don't sow, you will never reap." Hard to argue with that. At any rate, he left for Guatemala, basically penniless, and started serving on the mission field.

Central America was probably a perfect place for a laid-back guy like Doug, and he flourished there and became reasonably effective on the mission field. The senior pastor of our church at the time was so impressed that he decided to raise some funds to help Doug be more effective on the field. So, a year later, when Doug was home on furlough, our church presented him with a brand new four-wheel-drive truck. They drove it right into the sanctuary on a Sunday morning, to huge cheers from the congregation. It was very exciting and, are you ready for this? It was a Toyota truck. A Toyota! Just like the brand he had sowed, only new and not a piece of junk like his Corolla. I marvelled when I considered how Doug's simple faith was so effective that he would reap what he sowed. It is a principle I wish every person could experience firsthand so that they could begin to live life on a much higher economic basis.

> *The generous soul will be made rich,*
> *And he who waters will also be watered himself.*
>
> —Proverbs 11:25

Back in the day, we all wore suits on Sunday morning when we were in the pulpit. No self-respecting preacher would have been caught dead in a T-shirt and ripped jeans like they wear today. I remember one evening we were part of a city-wide gathering of some sort and a couple dozen of us pastors were all present in our Sunday morning best. Harold had shown up in the most dreadful brown wool suit I had seen in a long time. I recall thinking in my heart, "He really needs some new clothes."

Almost instantly, I felt like the Holy Spirit spoke to me and said, "You should give him one of yours."

I immediately thought, "Yeah, that's what I will do. I will give him that suit I don't wear any more. It's still in perfect shape and way better than the one he has on."

But again, I was prompted by the Holy Spirit, "No, give him your new one!"

This time I argued with the Lord, but He never argued back. I already knew the right thing to do was to sow your best seed. That's what farmers do; they plant their very best seed so as to ensure they get their very best harvest.

I had the suit, a classy double-breasted beauty, dry cleaned and delivered to him. It was a tough pill to swallow, actually. It was my favourite suit, and at my meager income, I would not be replacing it anytime soon.

About three months later, a young man in our congregation came up to me and asked me to meet him at his car. He said he had something for me. After the service I met him in the parking lot and he presented me with a stunning, custom tailored, double-breasted suit, along with the matching dress shirt and tie. He told me that he had bought the suit and only worn it once before he felt the Lord spoke to him and told him to give it to me. Then he told me that this had happened three months earlier but he had delayed because his wife did not want him to give it away. He further explained how, just that morning, his wife told him that the Lord had spoken to her that he needed to give me the suit.

At first, I felt awkward about the whole thing, but then I realized this was God's heavenly economy at work. I had sowed, and now I was reaping. He had sowed and would also reap. It was fascinating to me that I sowed my very best seed and I reaped something even better. It was a lesson that I have tried to never forget.

Passionate people overflow. They are contagious on every level and want to share what they have with others. The idea of *giving it away* should never be restricted to monetary things but applied to everything. There are three critical things that we should always consider giving away: our time, our talent and our treasure.

There is a serendipitous little detail in the story of Moses that many people miss. After Moses failed colossally as Pharaoh's stepson, he spent the next forty years in the back side of the desert, tending sheep. At eighty years old, he got a message from a burning bush to go back to Egypt and work on becoming a PHD (Potential Hebrew Deliverer). He was not sure he was up for the challenge and felt he was woefully ill-equipped. The Lord said, "What is that in your hand?" And he said, "A rod" (Exodus 4:2). Then the Lord told him to cast it to the ground, and when he did, it turned into a serpent.

The whole point of this exchange was that what he had in his hand was an ordinary thing, but if he laid it down, it would become something extraordinary. This is all any of us have to lay down or give away—something ordinary—but when we do, it is transformed into something more significant.

Moses's rod was a symbol. It represented his time, talent and treasure. His *time,* because he spent every waking moment using it to tend the sheep. His *talent,* because after forty years he was doubtless very good at using the staff to direct the sheep and ward off the predators. And finally, it represented his *treasure* because that was how he made his living. Just as Jesus transformed the disciples from fishers of fish to fishers of men, Moses was being transformed from leading sheep to leading men. But God needed him to lay down his time, talent and treasure to accomplish the task.

Retired newsman Dan Rather was on television one day lamenting the fact that volunteerism was way down in America.[96] He felt we were a more impoverished people for not being willing to do anything for others unless we are being paid. For many North Americans, their time has become their most valuable asset, and because most of us live ridiculously busy lives, we have become stingy with our time. We take this trend head-on in our church. We have recruited over one thousand volunteers, and they serve in every imaginable area. They have come to understand that God has given us everything, including our time, and it is our good pleasure to give Him something back.

Our staff are in a unique situation, in that all of them get paid to do what we ask others to do for free. So we constantly remind them that they,

---

[96] Eleanor Goldberg, "Volunteer Rates Hit All-Time Low" (*The Huffington Post*, April 10, 2014), https://www.huffingtonpost.com/2014/04/09/volunteer-rates-us_n_5113733.html.

too, should volunteer when the opportunity arises. For example, when we host an event to appreciate our volunteers, it is the staff who volunteers to serve them. One June, we were doing exactly that. Our sixty staff did all of the set-up for the event and served all the food. When the event was over, the volunteers went home feeling duly appreciated. The staff all stuck around to clean up the colossal mess we had made. I was collecting garbage and hauling it out to the dumpster. We had created so much trash that the bin was overflowing, so I climbed up into the dumpster and was jumping up and down on the garbage to create more space. Just then, Tracey, one of our volunteers who was late in departing, walked by to see me. "What on earth are you doing, Pastor Mark?" she shouted.

"I'm stomping down the garbage," I explained.

"No. I mean why are *you* doing it?" she incredulously queried.

"Because I'm on garbage duty," I offhandedly explained. She stood there watching for a couple of more minutes and made her way to her car. I never thought anything of it. The next day she sent me an email saying how she had never seen anything like it—a senior pastor of a megachurch stomping down the garbage in a dumpster. She explained how she was contemplating taking a picture of her senior pastor dumpster diving but decided it would have been inappropriate. (I would not have cared.) Then she thanked me for leading by example and being willing to do even the dirtiest job myself.

Anybody who has ever read John 11, where Jesus washes the feet of the disciples, will know that there should never be any job beneath any of us. There is a point not to be missed here: the reason we have one thousand volunteers is that those of us who lead, do so by example, and in the end, we reap what we sow. Every leader of every company, organization or family needs to learn this incredible principle of laying down our time for others.

In Chapter Sixteen, we looked at how people always get rewarded for exceptional talent. That, however, doesn't mean we should never give our skills away. In the greater scheme of things, our talent is a gift from God in the first place. Whatever potential and aptitude we possess was first implanted in us by God at the foundation of the world. One of the biggest mistakes we can make is to horde the gift. Again, it comes back down to sowing our best seed. Sure, it is great when we are paid well for what we do well, but what an honour it is to be able to give it away to a purpose greater than ourselves!

As mentioned earlier, I grew up in a lawyer's home. My father made a very good income and my mother was a sixties-style stay-at-home mom. That meant that, though she did not have a career of her own, she was regularly out and about, volunteering at church, school or the Junior League. One day, I was driving along with my dad and I asked him why he never volunteered like my mother. He casually answered, "Let me show you something," and we turned off our regular route and were going down a street I had never been down before. He stopped the car right in front of a Kiwanis retirement home and we went in. I had no idea what was going on and why we were at an "old folks" home. Purposefully, he led me down a long corridor and we stopped and, without saying a word, he pointed to a plaque on the wall. It read: *In recognition of J Barry Hughes QC for generously donating the legal services necessary to build this facility.* He never told anybody about this, but throughout his entire career as a lawyer, he always did legal work for charities for free. All the years he had been talking about doing *pro bono* work I thought it meant he was a big fan of the lead singer of U2. (Sorry couldn't resist.) He explained to me that he could typically charge a client two hundred dollars an hour. Then he asked me this question, "What do you think is a better donation, to come here and sweep the floor for ten hours or give them ten hours of free legal work?" I was never very good at math, but the answer was obvious.

It was a great lesson for me to learn as a child. We all have God given gifts that we can strategically sow into the lives of other people. It is hard for me to quantify exactly how that comes back to us, but I know that it does. The givers in this world are surrounded by others who generously open up their hearts to serve them as well.

If we truly want to live large in life, one of the ways of doing it is by becoming an exceedingly generous person. Whether our treasure is small or great, we can all be those who can discover the joy of giving it away.

Chapter Eighteen

The Windows of Heaven

I would not give one moment of heaven for all the joy and riches of the world.
—Martin Luther

For all of Solomon's wisdom, he was guilty of a classic mistake that has been repeated millions of times since the day man was chased out of the Garden of Eden. He tried to recreate heaven on this side of heaven by laying up treasures on earth!

I made my works great, I built myself houses, and planted myself vineyards. I made myself gardens and orchards, and I planted all kinds of fruit trees in them. I made myself water pools from which to water the growing trees of the grove. I acquired male and female servants, and had servants born in my house. Yes, I had greater possessions of herds and flocks than all who were in Jerusalem before me. I also gathered for myself silver and gold and the special treasures of kings and of the provinces. I acquired male and female singers, the delights of the sons of men, and musical instruments of all kinds. So I became great and excelled more than all who were before me in Jerusalem. Also my wisdom remained with me.

Whatever my eyes desired I did not keep from them. I did not withhold my heart from any pleasure, For my heart rejoiced in all my labor; And this was my reward from all my labor. Then I looked on all the works that my hands had done And on the labor in which I had toiled; And indeed all was vanity and grasping for the wind. There was no profit under the sun.

—Ecclesiastes 2:4–11

We are all guilty of this to some small degree. Everything in creation was put here to point us to the Creator. But the idolatry of man has continually been to worship the creation instead of the Creator. We desperately seek our little piece of the paradise in the form of wealth, property or things, forgetting that one day it will all pass away; we only have it on loan for a few very brief years. Since we were created to live in paradise, and one day will again, our heart longs for that state. Paul David Tripp, in his devotional *New Morning Mercies*, puts it this way;

> Here's the real-life, street-level issue: if you don't keep the eyes of your heart focused on the paradise that is to come, you will try to turn this poor fallen world into the paradise it will never be. In the heart of every living person is the longing for paradise... When you forget this you work very hard to try to turn this moment into the paradise it will never be. Your marriage will not be paradise. Your job will not be the paradise you long for. Your friendships will not be the paradise your heart craves. Your children will not deliver paradise to you. Even your church will not live up to the standard of paradise. If you're God's child, paradise has been guaranteed for you, but it will not be right here, right now. All the things that disappoint you now are to remind you that this is not all there is and to cause you to long for the paradise that is to come.[97]

Rather than being content to wait for heaven, Solomon committed his life's work to attempting to build paradise on earth. He spent his life seeking pleasure and possessions and carving out the most beautiful and richly adorned human kingdom ever known to man. He used his superior wisdom to amass his own personal fortune rather than use it to pursue the greater good, which was his original calling. Solomon realized, in the end, that it was nothing compared to eternity, but by then it was a little late. He had twelve thousand horses and 1,400 chariots. An archeological dig

---

[97] Paul David Tripp, *New Morning Mercies: A Daily Gospel Devotional*, 1st ed. (Wheaton, IL: Crossway Books, 2014), March 11 entry.

discovered one of his stables alone held 450 horses. Even Jay Leno doesn't have that many vehicles in his garage.

There are a few sins in the Western church that we have somehow convinced ourselves are actually virtues, not vices. Greed is certainly among them. South of our border, some preachers have taken the American dream, wrapped it in the gospel and convinced millions that God's will for their life is to be rich, fat and happy. There are North American preachers who live in ten-million-dollar homes and own a whole fleet of personal jets. I don't think it is unkind or critical to ask the question: Is this really necessary for the furtherance of the gospel? Should pastors, even highly successful ones, be living the same lifestyles as flamboyant rap artists?

Solomon's father David warned us not to be impressed with those who have amassed wealth and splendour on earth.

> *Do not be overawed when a man grows rich,*
>   *when the splendor of their houses increases;*
> *for they will take nothing with them when they die,*
>   *their splendor will not descend with them.*
> *Though while they live he counted themselves blessed—*
>   *and people praise you when you prosper—*
> *they will join those who have gone before them,*
>   *who will never see the light of life.*
> *People who have wealth but lack understanding*
>   *are like the beasts that perish.*
>
> —Psalm 49:16–20 NIV

Over the years, I have been vocally critical of preachers and pastors who live like they are rock stars or movie stars. Some of America's biggest-name preachers live in mansions, drive Rolls-Royces and fly multimillion-dollar private jets. They seem to have no trouble justifying their lifestyles and are genuinely surprised when others don't see it the same way.

One particular prosperity preacher sent a letter to his partners, asking them to donate three hundred dollars each so he could buy a sixty-five-million-dollar Gulfstream G650 plane. (I guess he banged up his previous jet on a botched landing.) The G650 was the latest and greatest in the world of private jets, flown by multinationals like Walmart and Exxon and billionaires like Warren Buffet and Oprah Winfrey. It cruises at seven hundred mph and is the ultimate in luxurious private jets. Somehow, our humble brother felt it was necessary for him to join the in-crowd of the ultra-rich. He already owned not one, but two Rolls-Royces. At any rate, the Christian community, to their credit, did not respond favourably to the campaign, and the fundraiser was quickly withdrawn. Still, he was outwardly angry about it and went on air attacking his critics and claiming they don't understand the Bible.

> "See, don't get upset when the world says stuff and talks about stuff, and all that. They're just looking through the wrong lens; they don't understand," he said in a sermon. "'What does a preacher need with an airplane?' They don't know," he added. "They'll never know because they're not looking through the Word. They will never know, never, never know."[98]

He's exactly right. I will never, never know.

Years ago, I was at a pastors conference where one of the speakers had the dubious nickname The Prophet of Prosperity. After hearing him speak, I was certain they had misspelled "prophet" and meant to use the more apt alternative "profit." In his "sermon" he described the quality of his suit and shoes, along with an elaborate explanation of the importance of a ten-thousand-dollar diamond tie pin, and then he spent the rest of the message talking about his car… which was a Rolls-Royce—you know, the luxury car that the Queen of England pulls out for special occasions. After describing the beryl wood dash and aluminum body panels, he made this bizarre statement: "Where do you think a design for a car like this comes… the pit of hell?" He was suggesting, of course, that anything so beautiful could have only come from heaven. His thesis was that the

---

[98] Yesha Callahan, "Creflo Dollar Is Still Whining About a Jet; Says Only Those Who Don't Understand the Bible Have an Issue," The Grapevine (The Root, January 12, 2017), https://thegrapevine.theroot.com/creflo-dollar-is-still-whining-about-a-jet-says-only-t-1790886922.

design for a Rolls-Royce was divine and that it was exactly the kind of car Jesus would drive in heaven (if He actually needed a car), and therefore, we should do likewise on earth. His proof text for this outrageous point was 1 John 4:17: *"…as He is, so are we in this world."* I AM NOT MAKING THIS STORY UP!

First off, he absolutely butchered the hermeneutic of that scripture and used the verse completely out of context. John is specifically and definitively talking about love, not cars or things. In other words, as Christ loves us, we should love one another, because as He is, so are we in this world. Not complicated stuff. Nevertheless, after thirty minutes or so of this, I was tangibly aggravated and ready to spit, gag or maybe even throw up. He knew he had provoked a few of the more thinking people in the crowd (the mindless lemmings were already shouting "Amen"). Then he made this statement: "Some of you are thinking, 'Show me a scripture that says Jesus drives a Rolls-Royce.' I say to you, show me one that says He doesn't." Did I mention that I am not making this up?

At this point, I did something I have never done before or since and hope I never do again. I stood up and, in a spirit of righteous contempt, said, "The Scripture says He rides a white horse," and walked out of the meeting. Because there were two thousand people in the room and I didn't shout it, the speaker did not hear me, but those sitting around me did. In retrospect, I am glad I didn't say it louder and make a scene, as it was not my place to correct him publicly. There was no need to add my insolence to his arrogance.

Jesus hasn't always ridden a white horse (Revelation 19:11). While He was stationed on earth, most of the time He walked. This was His chosen mode of transportation and it once caused Him to be four days late for a friend's funeral (John 11:17). Maybe His Rolls was in the shop. "Show me a scripture that says it wasn't!" (Sarcasm) On the rare occasion when Jesus did need proper transportation, He rode a donkey (Matthew 21)… and it was borrowed. Is there any way for us to even imagine the earthbound Jesus driving a Rolls, flying a private jet or living in a palatial mansion?

Matthew 8:20 answers the question: *"And Jesus said to him, 'Foxes have holes and birds of the air have nests, but the Son of Man has nowhere to lay His head.'"* Why did the King of Kings and Lord of Lords live like a pauper on earth? I am convinced it was to model to humanity the greater passion—a passion for the Kingdom of God, not the kingdom of this world. He doesn't want us to get so caught up in the things of this world that we end up missing the splendour of the next one.

> *So why do you worry about clothing? Consider the lilies of the field, how they grow: they neither toil nor spin; and yet I say to you that even Solomon in all his glory was not arrayed like one of these. Now if God so clothes the grass of the field, which today is, and tomorrow is thrown into the oven, will He not much more clothe you, O you of little faith? Therefore do not worry, saying, "What shall we eat?" or "What shall we drink?" or "What shall we wear?" For after all these things the Gentiles seek. For your heavenly Father knows that you need all these things. But seek first the kingdom of God and His righteousness, and all these things shall be added to you.*
> —Matthew 6:28–33

The Rolls-Royce example is, of course, ridiculous and a moot point for almost every one of us. Still, we all have a difficult time not comparing ourselves to others. It is not like we measure ourselves against the Rothschilds or the Rockefellers; we tend to struggle with comparing ourselves with the people across the street who own a better car or a better lawnmower. You've all seen the TV commercials where Bill next door is ripping around the yard with his new turbo charged Toro riding lawn mower. It's got electronic fuel injection and hydrostatic drive. And you are still starting yours by pulling a rope and pushing it through the grass—what a loser!

I am not suggesting that we should not own a car or a house, or even a plane, for that matter. What I am suggesting is that heaven can wait. We will one day live in mansions that will make Buckingham Palace look like a dump. We are not called to try to recreate heaven on earth. Any attempt to do so will cause us to miss the greater purpose.

Here is what Jesus instructed us to do with our treasure:

Do not lay up for yourselves treasures on earth, where moth and rust destroy and where thieves break in and steal; but lay up for yourselves treasures in heaven, where neither moth nor rust destroys and where thieves do not break in and steal. For where your treasure is, there your heart will be also.

—Matthew 6:19–21

When we give away our finances, some of us make the mistake of thinking that's the end of it, that it is gone until we get to heaven… where, frankly, we don't really need it since the streets are paved with gold anyway. What good does my fifty dollars do there? The Scripture never says we cannot access our heavenly bank account while here on earth. In fact, it says the opposite.

"Will a man rob God? Yet you have robbed Me! But you say, 'In what way have we robbed You?' In tithes and offerings. You are cursed with a curse, For you have robbed Me, Even this whole nation. Bring all the tithes into the storehouse, That there may be food in My house, And try Me now in this," Says the Lord of hosts, "If I will not open for you the windows of heaven And pour out for you such blessing That there will not be room enough to receive it. And I will rebuke the devourer for your sakes, So that he will not destroy the fruit of your ground, Nor shall the vine fail to bear fruit for you in the field," Says the Lord of hosts; "And all nations will call you blessed, For you will be a delightful land," Says the Lord of hosts.

—Malachi 3:8–12

First, God says that those who do not pay Him a tithe (ten percent of their income) He considers as thieves. This goes back to a previous point: it all belongs to Him anyway. Worse yet, we live under a financial curse when we are not givers. It is not to say that God curses us but that our money is caught in the capricious grip of the world's economy, which in the end, will betray all of us and steal everybody's wealth.[99]

On the other hand, God Himself promises to look after the abundant giver and *"to open for you the windows of heaven and pour out for you such blessing that there will not be room enough to receive it."* There it is! He promises that He will open the heavenly bank account and pour it back onto you here on earth.

The Scripture never says we cannot access our heavenly bank account while here on earth. In fact, it says the opposite.

The expression "open the windows of heaven" appears in only one other place in Scripture. It is in Genesis 7, during the days of Noah, when God flooded the entire earth with water. It says that *"the windows of heaven were opened"*(v. 11) and it rained for forty days and forty nights. The imagery should not be lost on us that this is the kind of largesse that God wants to bestow on the generous giver.

And if that were not enough, He kicks it up another notch by saying he will also *"rebuke the devourer for your sakes."* The people of Malachi's day know exactly what he was talking about. In their agricultural economy, the devourer could have been drought, plant disease, fungus, or pestilence such as insects and locusts. They were all too familiar with

---

[99] Revelation 18:10–11 predicts that the world's economy will eventually collapse in one hour. "'Alas, alas, that great city Babylon, that mighty city! For in one hour your judgment has come.' And the merchants of the earth will weep and mourn over her, for no one buys their merchandise anymore." We had a harbinger of this on September 14, 2008,* when Lehman Bros declared intent to declare bankruptcy. Four days later, by 11 a.m. the sell orders on the money market had hit $550 billion. The Federal Reserve stepped in and stopped the drawdown with a guarantee of $250,000 per account to prevent further panic. By the Fed's own estimation, if it had not stepped in by 2 p.m. the draw down would have reached $5.5 trillion and the electronic run on the banks would have caused the collapse of the US economy. By the next day world's economic system as we know it would have come to an end. For the general population, most didn't even realize that it had happened. (*These details were a direct quote from a C-Span video I viewed, but it has now been removed from YouTube and C-Span. Ref. https://www.liveleak.com/view?i=ca2_1234032281.

these things and were engaged in a constant battle against crop failure, not unlike farmers are today, yet with no pesticides to combat them. So God promised them that He Himself would rebuke the devourer and ensure that the ground would be fruitful. For most of us, the devourer looks a little different today. It could be the car breaking down, the washing machine quitting or the hot water tank bursting. These annoying little things are capable of eating away at our finances so that we feel like what Haggai describes: *"And he who earns wages, Earns wages to put into a bag with holes"* (Haggai 1:6). We have a more modern idiom: "His money is burning a hole in his pocket." When the children of Israel wandered in the desert for forty years, neither their shoes nor their clothes wore out. I can't imagine any woman being happy with wearing the same outfit for forty years, but I guess you could argue there was no way for it to go out of style.

I have done a bit of a real-life experiment on this. And, no, I did not wear a veteran pair of underwear for forty years. (My oldest pair is maybe only twenty-seven.) What I did do was try to see how long I could drive the same vehicle. In the last four decades, I have only had four vehicles. I have driven every one of them in excess of 300,000 kilometers. This is an incredible feat in a country where they dump tons of salt on the streets every winter. I had a 1997 Pontiac Transport with a plastic body that did not rust. I drove that vehicle to 450,000 km and then gave it to my brother-in-law, who drove it up to 500,000 km. Even until last year, when people in our congregation would see me roll into the parking lot with my then seventeen-year-old minivan with 350,000 km, they would point at me and laugh. Some have wondered aloud whether maybe they are not paying me enough. Maybe my encounter with the Prophet of Prosperity has made me too cynical on this subject. At any rate, I am still making a point. God is able to take care of us and our stuff while we take care of His work on earth. We have always been able to support missions work around the world because we have not been consumed with spending our money on ourselves.

In the interests of full disclosure, I probably need to tell one more story on this. One Sunday morning, I was preaching on the passage from Malachi 3 and making the point empathically that God will rebuke the devourer. That day, I chose the example of the hot water tank bursting. I humorously made the point that it was the least fun way to spend one thousand dollars. One day you have hot water, the next day you have hot water all over the basement floor. You call someone, give them one thousand dollars, and you have hot water again. The tank doesn't look any different than the last one. You cannot take it to the golf course and enjoy it like a new set of clubs. It just sits in the basement and makes hot water and steals your hard-earned one thousand dollars. As I gave the illustration, I got a few chuckles, as every homeowner in the room got the point—they had all been there at one time or another.

But here's where the story gets weird. I got home from church that day to find my basement flooded with water from a burst hot water tank. I could scarcely believe my eyes. Of all days for this to happen, it happened on the very day I used it as an illustration. After I gave someone my one thousand dollars, I scratched my head as to how this could have happened. In the end, I came to realize a hot water tank only lasts ten years. That is just the way it is. I could still celebrate the fact that it didn't quit just one day after the five-year warranty expired.

In the greater scheme of things, God has been immensely faithful to us and we have had little in the way of disastrous expenses that sometime befall people. If we will boldly honour God with our finances, He can and He will bless us beyond what we can imagine.

John Wesley was arguably one of the most influential people of all time. He and his brother Charles founded Methodism in the eighteenth century. Charles was the musician and penned 6,500 hymns while John was the preacher. John Wesley rode over 250,000 miles on horseback, a distance equal to ten trips around the equator. He preached three times a day, seven days a week, well into his eighties. It is estimated that he preached forty thousand sermons and still managed to publish four hundred different works on a broad range of subjects from theology to medicine to prose.

After graduating from Oxford, Wesley was offered a teaching position with the venerable university in 1729. His annual salary was a handsome thirty British pounds, more than enough for a single man to live on. Even after paying all his living expenses of twenty-eight pounds, he found he had a surplus and decided to use it to purchase some pictures to decorate his flat. Shortly thereafter, the chambermaid came in to do the housekeeping and she was wearing no coat, even though it was the middle of winter. Wesley regretted that he had spent his abundance on himself and that he had nothing with which to help those in need.

The next year his income doubled to sixty pounds, but this time he lived on the twenty-eight and gave thirty-two to poor. By year three, he was earning ninety pounds and was able to give away sixty-two. This pattern continued for his entire life until, one year, he earned 1,400 pounds and was still only living on roughly thirty pounds while giving the rest away.

John Wesley believed that followers of Christ should always increase their standard of *giving*, not their standard of *living*.[100] In 1744 he wrote, "[When I die] if I leave behind me ten pounds… you and all mankind [may] bear witness against me, that I have lived and died a thief and a robber."[101] When he died in 1791, the only money mentioned in his will was the miscellaneous coins to be found in his pockets and dresser drawers. It is estimated that he gave away thirty thousand pounds in his lifetime. My calculations put that somewhere over five million dollars in today's money.

Don't forget that he would have had to earn all that money to have given it away. By anyone's standards, he was a very wealthy man. His simple motto for money was this, "Earn all you can, give all you can, save all you can."[102] That stands in stark contrast to the motto in our materialistic world today that says, "Get all you can, can all you get and sit on the can."

---

[100] Charles Edward White, "What Wesley Practiced and Preached About Money," CT Pastors (*Leadership Journal*, July 25, 2018), https://www.christianitytoday.com/pastors/1987/winter/87l1027.html.

[101] Ibid.

[102] John Wesley, "17 Christian Quotes & Sayings by John Wesley" (All Christian Quotes), accessed June 5, 2020, https://www.allchristianquotes.org/authors/11/John_Wesley.

Chapter Nineteen

Crossing the Finish Line

Beginning in itself has no value, it is an end which makes beginning meaningful, we must end what we begun.

—Amit Kalantri

In 1992, British track star Derek Redmond was the fastest man on the planet. He had won the 1991 World Championships for the four-hundred-metre race and was the favourite to win the gold medal at the Barcelona Olympics. He posted the fastest time of the first round and went on to win his quarter-final. In the semi-final, Redmond started well, but just over halfway, in the back straight away, he tore his hamstring. He knew what had happened and hobbled to a halt, and then he fell to the ground in pain. The stretcher bearers made their way over to him, but he waved them off. Redmond decided he wanted to finish the race. He got up and began to hobble along the track, clearly in extreme pain. His father, Jim Redmond, who had been sitting in the stands, barged past the security guards to join his son on the track. Jim put his arm around his son Derek and together the two of them completed the lap around the track. As they crossed the finish line, the crowd of 65,000 spectators rose to their feet to give Derek a standing ovation. No one seemed to pay any attention to the athlete who had actually won the race. Even to this day, when people recall the Barcelona games, they remember Derek Redmond, and not American Quincy Watts who had just set a new Olympic record and went on to win the gold medal.

Because Redmond was assisted by his father, he was officially disqualified and Olympic records state that he "Did Not Finish." Nevertheless, the moment has gone down in history as one of the most memorable ever and later became the subject of one of the International Olympic Committee's "Celebrate Humanity" videos, which proclaimed: "Force is measured in kilograms. Speed is measured in seconds. Courage? You can't measure courage."

In 2008, Redmond was featured in a series of Visa credit card commercials promoting the Olympic Games. The iconic moment was narrated by actor Morgan Freeman noting, "He and his father finished dead last, but he and his father finished."[103]

For all of King Solomon's wisdom and achievements, he did not finish well. He began his run with such great potential. His original intent was to use his exceptional giftedness to lead the people of Israel. When God made the offer to ask whatever he wanted, Solomon responded with extreme humility, claiming he was but a mere child who did not have the wherewithal to lead such a great people. *"For who is able to judge this great people of Yours?"* (1 Kings 3:9). The Lord took great pleasure in Solomon's humble answer and bestowed on him both great wisdom and wealth. So, it is disheartening to see how badly he misused it and how poorly he finished his course.

For it came to pass, when Solomon was old, that his wives turned away his heart after other gods: and his heart was not perfect with the Lord his God, as was the heart of David his father.

—1 Kings 11:4 KJV

Like many great leaders of history, Solomon was a victim of his own success and he fell prey to the proverbial allure of money, sex and power. With seven hundred wives and three hundred concubines, there can be no doubt that Solomon was a bona fide sex addict. And there is no question that he abused both his wealth and his power. If Solomon was unable to see his failings in his middle and final years, by the very end he had begun to see the light. He became convinced and arguably remorseful that he

---

[103] "Derek Redmond," Wikipedia (Wikimedia Foundation), accessed June 5, 2020, https://en.wikipedia.org/wiki/Derek_Redmond.

had failed miserably. In the book of Ecclesiastes he outlines an impressive array of personal accomplishments. He pursued and acquired every human desire that a man could possibly want, only to realize that there was no lasting value in it whatsoever and that, in fact, he had wasted his entire life chasing these things. Then, as he pondered the situation even more as to what he had done with his life, his heart fell into complete despair.

> *Therefore I hated life because the work that was done under the sun was distressing to me, for all is vanity and grasping for the wind. Then I hated all my labor in which I had toiled under the sun, because I must leave it to the man who will come after me. And who knows whether he will be wise or a fool? Yet he will rule over all my labor in which I toiled and in which I have shown myself wise under the sun. This also is vanity. Therefore I turned my heart and despaired of all the labor in which I had toiled under the sun.*
>
> —Ecclesiastes 2:17–20

Wow, imagine spending your entire life pursuing and achieving something, only to look back and literally despise what you have done because you realize how pointless it all was. Unfortunately, this dilemma is far from being for only the rich. We all struggle with the purpose of life and the possibility that we placed far too much importance on money, our occupations and our things.

When Solomon died, his son Rehoboam became king in his place. The people of Israel gathered to him and said,

> *Your father made our yoke heavy; now therefore, lighten the burdensome service of your father, and his heavy yoke which he put on us, and we will serve you.*
>
> —1 Kings 12:4

Unsure how to lead, Rehoboam consulted two different groups of advisors: first, the elders of his father's court; and then, the trust-fund, silver-spoon crowd of young men that he had grown up with lounging around the royal pool. This is what the elders said:

If you will be a servant to these people today, and serve them, and answer them, and speak good words to them, then they will be your servants forever.
—1 Kings 12:7

Then Rehoboam asked his young privileged friends the same question, to which they answered,

Thus you should speak to this people who have spoken to you, saying, "Your father made our yoke heavy, but you make it lighter on us"—thus you shall say to them: "My little finger shall be thicker than my father's waist! And now, whereas my father put a heavy yoke on you, I will add to your yoke; my father chastised you with whips, but I will chastise you with scourges!"
—1 Kings 12:10–11

As mentioned previously, Rehoboam sadly went with the advice of his younger peers and, within a few short years, destroyed everything that his forefathers David and Solomon spent a lifetime building. Just as tragically, the narrative also tells us that Solomon gained his wealth by chastising, whipping, and taxing his people half to death. He fell victim to the very dangers of wealth, of which he warned others in the Proverbs.

He who oppresses the poor to increase his riches, And he who gives to the rich, will surely come to poverty.
—Proverbs 22:16

The history books are full of stories like this, of leaders who came from humble beginnings but could not handle the responsibilities of wealth and power. Leonid Brezhnev was one such example. He was born into a simple Ukrainian family. After the Russian Revolution, he joined the communist party to fight for the socialist ideals of taking the wealth and power from the oligarchy and sharing it equally amongst the proletariat working class.

He rose through the ranks of the party, and by 1964, he had become the de facto leader of the USSR. He decorated his own uniform with over one hundred medals, which spawned a popular joke, "He had to have chest expansion surgery to make room for one more Gold Star medal."[104] He lived in a palatial estate with gardens and pools and a garage full of exotic cars, from Maseratis to Rolls-Royces, and even an American-made Cadillac that was a gift from US President Richard Nixon. One day Brezhnev was being visited by his aging mother and he proudly gave her a tour of his home and his estate and his garage full of expensive cars. When he asked her what she thought of all the wonderful things he had acquired, she became quite concerned and asked him, "But Leonid, what if the Communists find out?"

Today, it has become so common for people in power to be embroiled in scandal and corruption that we no longer even expect our leaders to adhere to a moral code. Almost no one expects politicians to keep their campaign promises. When the media points out the litany of broken promises, most people just shrug and wonder why anybody believed them in the first place. Corruption and compromise are not just commonplace among secular leaders but have become, unfortunately, almost as rampant amongst spiritual leaders. We hear of big-name ministers having affairs, divorcing their wives, misappropriating funds and abusing drugs and alcohol. I personally have had perhaps a dozen pastor friends that have crashed and burned in various ways over the years. Several compromised their integrity and their fidelity by falling headlong into adulterous affairs. Some of them carried on these double lives for years. They were one person in the pulpit and a completely different one in their private lives. It was duplicity at its very worst. Once the truth came out, which it always does, they lost their churches, their careers, their paycheques, their homes, their marriages and pretty much everything else they had spent their adult life building.

---

[104] Alice E. M. Underwood, "10 Things (And 5 Jokes) You Didn't Know About Brezhnev," *Russian Life*, accessed June 5, 2020, https://www.russianlife.com/stories/online/10-things-and-5-jokes-you-didn-t-know-about-brezhnev.

The Lord is actually far more interested in our success than we are, and if we are going to finish well in life we need to define a win.

Someone once said, "What we build with our gifting we can destroy in an instant with our character." Why do people think they live inside a vacuum? That they can carry on in whatever selfish way they wish without consequences? Everything we do affects other people—our spouse, our children, our friends, our employees, everyone within our circle of influence. Unless we live alone in a cave somewhere, we are all part of a community, and when we mess up, it messes everybody up. Jesus said, *"But whoever causes one of these little ones who believe in Me to stumble, it would be better for him if a millstone were hung around his neck, and he were thrown into the sea"* (Mark 9:42). Yikes! We should fear God way too much to be willing to live so carelessly and take such dangerous risks.

Again, this is the power of the dark side of passion; the very driven nature that motivates us to achieve can conspire against us to draw us into our sinful passions. Every time I witness this, I am just as shocked and dismayed as the time before. And I hope I never become so desensitized that I come to expect it. My most overwhelming emotion is the fear that I myself would succumb to such desires. After all, none of us are immune to temptations. Oscar Wilde mused, "I can resist anything except temptation." When we see others fail, even leaders, we need to remind ourselves that we are no better than they are. To think that any one of us is above temptation is a deception in itself. But for the grace of God, every one of us would end up a broken vessel, shipwrecked on the rocky shoals of life. Even Paul the apostle makes a striking claim that Jesus Himself had to battle the temptations of the flesh: *"For we do not have a High Priest who cannot sympathize with our weaknesses, but was in all points tempted as we are, yet without sin"* (Hebrews 4:15). It is hard to imagine, but if we are reading this correctly, we realize that even Jesus was tempted sexually like any other man. The big difference is that He did not succumb to the temptation.

It should not escape our notice that there are so many stories of failure in Scripture. If any of us were God and we were going to write a book about our "favourite people," the list would not likely include so many colossal screw-ups. But the bad examples are just as important as the good ones. What they do is clearly illustrate that bad behaviour has bad consequences. This is more helpful than we realize, as it reminds us that finishing well will not be a cake walk for any of us. It should also not escape our notice that virtually every one of them fell because they isolated themselves and did not walk in accountability to others. It doesn't really matter who we are; we are all weak and vulnerable human beings. The moment we think that we are above temptation is the moment we are at grave risk. The wiles of the enemy have taken down better people than the likes of us. Nobody stands alone. Nobody succeeds alone. Derek Redmond did not cross the finish line alone. He had help. God will always put others in our lives that will walk with us. And best of all, He Himself will step in and carry us across the finish line if we let Him.

The Lord is actually far more interested in our success than we are, and if we are going to finish well in life we need to define a win. Too often, we fail to measure accurately what a true win is. Too many people bump along in life and never pause long enough to ask the most important question: What would a win actually look like? What would we need to see happen to feel like we had crossed the finish line as a winner?

The apostle Paul passionately declared, *"I have fought the good fight, I have finished the race, I have kept the faith"* (2 Timothy 4:7). He doesn't tell us exactly what the win was for him, but whatever it was, he clearly felt like he had accomplished it. For each of us, the win is a subjective designation. Different people will apply different criteria. Every individual needs to decide this for themselves. For Derek Redmond, the win became just crossing the finish line. The gold medal had already vanished from sight. Given the circumstances, he had to redefine the win.

Many of us need to redefine the win. Like Solomon, we have been focused on the wrong thing for so long we are not even sure what success looks like.

When Billy Graham passed away in his one-hundredth year in 2018, it seemed like a cause for celebration. Not because he died—although at ninety-nine that is a celebration—but because he proved that a man could spend his entire life in ministry without a single scandal. That is not to say that he did not make mistakes, for we all do, but he left this earth without suffering a reproach or an embarrassment of his own making.

For every one of us, especially Christians, it is important to finish well. That is because our lives are on display for the whole world to see. People judge God by what they see us do. My pastor growing up used to say, "If you want to know how to live as a Christian, just ask a non-Christian." I have never forgotten that advice because it is so true. 2 Corinthians 3:2 put it this way: *"You are our epistle written in our hearts, known and read by all men…"*

So, what would a win look like for me? First and foremost, it would be more about relationships than about accomplishments. Here is my best shot at it. Hopefully it will be helpful as you define your own win.

- **Marriage**: A loving marriage that lasts a lifetime would be a big win. Our world desperately needs a few good examples as to what a marriage could be. I do not expect perfection, as that went out the window on day two of married life. We rocked day one, though!

- **Children and grandchildren** that all love Jesus, to me, would be the equivalent of an Olympic Gold Medal. I have told our congregation many times that I love them and want the best for them, but the fact that my own grown children all love God, love church life and serve Jesus in some way is my greatest joy.

- **Monetarily**: I don't mind if I am never rich, but I don't ever want to be stingy. If I did not have enough resources to be able to give to the work of the gospel or to another person in need, I would feel like I was poor. Being known as a generous person should be on everybody's list as a criterion of success.

- **Accomplishments:** Recognizable success is not anywhere near as important as whether I was faithful to what God asked me to do with my life. I worry a little bit about this because it is so easy to get distracted by my own selfish passions. *Who we are* is far more important than *what we do*,[105] but I really hope to hear the words, *"Well done, good and faithful servant… Enter into the joy of your Lord"* (Matthew 25:21).

- **Servant Leadership:** My hope would be that I would have lived my life as a servant leader and not a controlling autocrat. I would like to think that I could be the kind of leader that did everything he could to walk in integrity and not abuse the position God has put me in over other people.

- **Finishing Well:** Finally, if I could make it to the end of my life without a scandal of my own making and with my loyalty and good character intact, that would be a win. Someone once said that integrity is who you are when no one is looking. It is an excellent definition.

---

[105]   Mark Hughes, *A Greater Purpose*, 165.

Chapter Twenty

Conclusion

The world is changed by your example, not by your opinion.

—Paulo Coelho

We live in a world of people who are desperately lost in their distractions, their materialism and their hedonism. They are looking for something with meaning, and we can show it to them just by being the people God has called us to be.

The great irony is that, in our postmodern culture, we as Christians, and Evangelicals in particular, are bombarded with insults, calling us archaic, backward and repressive. But what pop culture, the media and academia repeatedly miss is the incalculable contribution that Christianity has made to the world through the hundreds of millions of rank and file Christians that simply live out their faith passionately. Who do they think is running food banks, homeless shelters, and soup kitchens in the inner cities? Who do they think is founding and funding the homes for orphans in the world's poorest countries? It is not some altruistic organization of atheists. It is the church! Who do they think is ministering to the incarcerated in prisons or running twelve-step programs for those trying to overcome drug and alcohol addictions? Alcoholics Anonymous was originally created by Bill Smith and Bob Wilson who, in the 1930s, discovered the twelve spiritual steps to recovery that only worked if one acknowledged God and asked Him for help.[106]

---

[106] "A History of the 12 Steps" (Cornerstone of Recovery, September 19, 2018), https://www.cornerstoneofrecovery.com/better-way-of-life-a-history-of-the-12-steps.

The same is true for the AIDS hospices around the world. In our city of Winnipeg, the only hospice for AIDS victims is run by Christian people,[107] and our church has been supporting them financially from their beginning. After Rick Warren's book *The Purpose Driven Life* became an international bestseller, he began to give away his millions of dollars in royalties. One of his most passionate initiatives was the fight against AIDS/HIV and he has become a worldwide champion for the cause.[108] For the last 350 years, the Catholic and Protestant churches have established thousands of hospitals around the world so that regular people would have access to healthcare which, historically, was only available to the rich.[109] When missionary David Livingstone left for Africa in 1840, he first went to medical school so that he could bring the people of that continent not only the gospel but also modern medicine.[110] He established both hospitals and schools wherever he went and recorded lower mortality rates than Western hospitals.

The public school system, which slowly emerged in developed countries, was almost always a result of the efforts of Christians. In Canada, Methodist minister Egerton Ryerson is considered *the father of the public school system* because of his tireless work in Ontario in the mid-eighteen hundreds to give all children access to an education.[111] Around the same period in the United Kingdom, it was missionary George Müller who not only cared for over ten thousand orphans but established 117 schools and

107 Leah Janzen, "'House of Mercy' Comforts AIDS Victims ," *The Winnipeg Free Press*, September 18, 2004. Retrieved June 5, 2020 online from https://s3.amazonaws.com/media.cloversites.com/6d/6d2285a4-c72b-4686-8851-865117a7a1c3/documents/House_of_Mercy.pdf

108 Outreach Media Group (Lindy Lowry), "Rick Warren on the AIDS Crisis," churchleaders.com, September 22, 2010, https://churchleaders.com/outreach-missions/outreach-missions-articles/139413-rick-warren-on-outreach.html.

109 "History of Hospitals," Wikipedia (Wikimedia Foundation, May 3, 2020), https://en.wikipedia.org/wiki/History_of_hospitals#Church-sponsored_hospitals_and_nurses.

110 Biography.com Editors, "David Livingstone," The Biography.com website (A&E Television Networks, May 14, 2019), https://www.biography.com/people/david-livingstone-9383955.

111 Neil Semple, "Egerton Ryerson," The Canadian Encyclopedia (Historica Canada, July 27, 2017), https://www.thecanadianencyclopedia.ca/en/article/egerton-ryerson.

educated 120,000 children.[112] Virtually every one of the most prestigious institutions of higher learning such as Yale, Harvard and Princeton were begun as religious schools to train young people for life and ministry.[113] Even in my own city, the University of Winnipeg was founded by the Methodists as a seminary in 1888 and called Wesley College.[114]

It was Christians that brought an end to the legal human slave trade in the world. People like William Wilberforce, a British MP who was converted to Christ shortly after being elected and who discovered his God given purpose and passion in life was to end human slavery. He relentlessly battled for forty-six years against one of the most powerful industries of his day. Finally, in 1833, just three days before his death, he received the news that the slaves had been emancipated.[115] The personal and political price he paid for his efforts was extraordinary, but he was able to leave this world with the confidence that his was a life well lived.

Nowhere in the world do women enjoy more freedoms and equal rights with their male counterparts than they do in Christendom. With all the empty rants we hear against the Christian faith and the repression of females, nothing could be further from the truth. At the time of Jesus, women in virtually every known culture were little more than possessions, and in many cases they were treated no better than slaves. Jesus began a revolution that liberated and empowered woman. The entire gospel story revolves around the heroism of Elizabeth, Mary, Martha and Mary, Mary Magdalene and others. Even within the early church, women rose

---

112   Ed Stetzer, "Prayer, Happiness and Communion with God (George Muller)," The Exchange with Ed Stetzer (Christianity Today International, July 12, 2011), https://www.christianitytoday.com/edstetzer/2011/july/prayer-happiness-and-communion-with-god-george-muller.html.

113   "Ivy League," Wikipedia (Wikimedia Foundation, May 17, 2020), https://en.wikipedia.org/wiki/Ivy_League.

114   Gordon Goldsborough, "Historic Sites of Manitoba: Wesley College / United College / University of Winnipeg (505 Portage Avenue, Winnipeg)," Manitoba Historical Society (Manitoba Historical Society, page revised January 13, 2020), http://www.mhs.mb.ca/docs/sites/wesleycollege.shtml.

115   Jon Bloom, "The Darling Object of William Wilberforce," desiringGod.org (Desiring God, February 24, 2012), https://www.desiringgod.org/articles/the-darling-object-of-william-wilberforce.

to places of extraordinary leadership and, like Priscilla and Junia, were named among the Apostles.[116]

> *There is neither Jew nor Greek, there is neither slave nor free, there is neither male nor female; for you are all one in Christ Jesus.*
>
> —Galatians 3:28

We could talk about the contributions of Christians to science, and literature, and art, and politics, and architecture, and music, and a hundred other disciplines, but that would require an entire book in itself. The Church, through its faith-filled, passion-driven adherents, has done more for the good of the human race than all other groups of people put together, and we are arguably the only real moral voice left in the world. Our generation has become sexually obsessed, morally bankrupt and verbally foul. If we were to just "shut up" or "disappear" like our critics demand, our world would spiral down to the abyss in a heartbeat.

Anyone who is unclear as to whether we have a part to play in all this needs to think again. If we will *delight ourselves in the Lord,* He will place within our hearts the greater passion—a passion to make a difference in our world and to leave it a better place than when we found it.

Every one of us has been placed on earth with a God-given destiny, and He desires to fuel that purpose with a God-given passion

---

The church is one of the places where people have an opportunity to discover their greater passion. This is because we don't exist for ourselves but to fulfil the call of Jesus and the mission of the gospel. The church is a group of ordinary people that come together to do extraordinary things. We heal peoples' lives and marriages, feed the poor, send missionaries around the world, build orphanages, plant churches, minister to the needs of the inner city, and on and on. The work is endless and sometimes

---

[116] Romans 6:3, 7

thankless, but the reward is great in heaven because we have been called to make a difference in the lives of others.

Every one of us has been placed on earth with a God-given destiny, and He desires to fuel that purpose with a God-given passion—the passion that comes from above, not the selfish unreliable ones that come only from within. Then, and only then, can we align our greater passion with our greater purpose, which ultimately produces our greatest fulfilment in life.

If we can define the win around those two things, then we have found the ultimate combination. If we can just drag ourselves away from the TV, or the cell phone, or the computer screen, or the golf course (or whatever our greater preoccupation is), then we can focus on becoming passionate spouses, parents, friends, Christians, teachers, researchers, professionals, influencers and world changers.

Oh, that every one of us would strive to finish the journey well, to leave behind a positive legacy for those who follow behind us and be able to say we lived without regret! *"If God is for us, who can be against us?"* (Romans 8:31). We can all learn to live large in life and love because *"He who is in us is greater than he who is in the world"* (1 John 4:4).